# StarMatter

Towards a new perspective

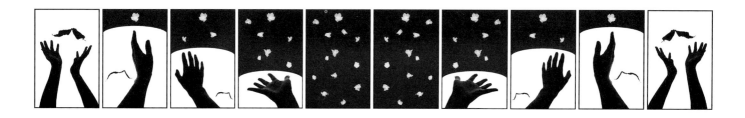

## The Graphics

The graphics comprise five basic images. When put in sequence they tell a short story, that of day becoming night and the following dawn. Through symbols and hand gestures the concepts of StarMatter and Deep Time are introduced. Their story can be mimicked by casting shadows on a wall, a visual exercise that could be used for example to teach these concepts to children. The graphics may be read separately from the text while leafing through the book.

First in the sequence are two hands. They are playing with a bird. A star appears and one of the hands reaches up with interest. Darkness gathers and stars begin to crowd the sky. Confused the hand pulls back but night continues to fall, down and down, pushing against the hand, crushing. There is no escape. Eventually, only the stars are left, shining out cold and bright.

Reversal of the image sequence tells the story of daybreak. It produces the opposite emotional effect, leaving a very positive and childlike impression. This time we start with night. A hand appears and begins to push up the darkness. Night lifts and starts to disappear. The hand bids farewell. Then, as if lonely, it reaches out to try and grasp the last fading star. But the sky fills with light and the star disappears. Instead the hands catch a bird and they start to play.

The aim is to show a simple human story, the hands symbolizing mankind, and the bird flying through the images marking time. The cycle between night and day puts the story on a scale we feel we should understand but nonetheless one that the hands seem to be unaware of. Their struggle and hope in the face of the inevitable is perhaps a parallel

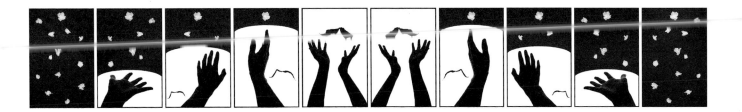

of our own search for greater awareness. Daybreak is a very meagre interval of time when measured against the universe, but it's what we know and so a place to start from.

The layout design echoes this cycle and also makes clear a greater context: our place in the universe. Single images build up to form a sequence, and then this sequence is mirrored and multiplied to form a *'star'*, which is in turn copied and recopied until it creates an impression of space. All this shows where in the story we are, and places the single image within the bigger picture.

The front cover is a collage of these graphics and is built on three planes of interpretation, or depth. First, in the foreground there is a hand reaching towards a red *'star'*. The arch that separates them represents the division between Earth and space, or perhaps the division between our immediate reality and a greater awareness. Second, behind this hand, a patchwork of *'stars'* floats by. The human story as told above is encapsulated within each of these *'stars'*, illustrating the concept that we, and everything, are made from stardust. Third, in the distant background, there are still more *'stars'*. This time they are so far away that they only figure as dots, much like the real stars we see in our own night sky. Do they tell the same story as the near stars? Do they even still exist? Perhaps all we are looking at is their light travelling through time... deep time.

Gavin Frankel    Paris 2004

# StarMatter

## Towards a new perspective

Contributors

Leslie Brown

Gordon MacLellan

Tom Mason

Chris Vis

This project is dedicated to the world's children

StarMatter  Towards a new perspective

Copyright © 2005 Leslie Brown, Gordon MacLellan, Tom Mason and Chris Vis.

First published in 2005 by StillWell, P.O.Box 5367, London W1A 2WT.

Leslie Brown, Gordon MacLellan, Tom Mason and Chris Vis assert the moral right to be identified as the authors of this work.

A CIP catalogue record of this title is available from the British Library.

ISBN 0-9550345-0-7

Designed and typeset by Black Mountain Design, Dublin.

Printed in the UK by St. Edmundsbury Press, Bury St. Edmunds.

## Acknowledgments

It would be impossible to list all the individuals and organisations who have given so freely of their time and expertise to assist in the compilation of this complex and ground-breaking work.

The authors extend their sincere thanks to all who have shared their enthusiasm and faith in the StarMatter project.

## Disclaimer

While every effort has been made to ensure the accuracy of the information herein, we do not hold ourselves responsible for any inadvertent errors.  Neither the authors nor the publishers can accept responsibility for any loss occasioned to any person, howsoever caused, or arising as a result of, or in consequence of action taken or refrained from in reliance on the contents of this work.  The listing of a person or organization in any part of this work does not imply any form of endorsement by the authors or the publishers of the material, products or services provided by that person or organization. Similarly, links to other websites have been inserted for your convenience and do not constitute endorsement of material at those sites, or any associates' organization, product or service.

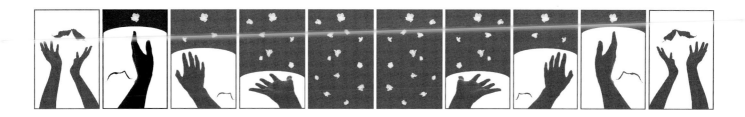

## Synopsis

StarMatter offers concepts and ideas for developing an awareness and appreciation of where we came from and where we are going. It discusses some of the big questions that historically have occupied our minds as a species, yet is broader in scale and sweep than just science.

The approach adopted is *non-human centred* with explanation of such fascinating concepts and systems as *Deep Time*, the planets, stars and the origin of matter that even we humans are composed of. These concepts are portrayed through the arts thus encouraging scientific discipline and the arts to be viewed as allies, not adversaries. The work is aimed at anyone interested in understanding ourselves, our world, its history, and our place in the universe.

StarMatter contains fascinating facts and ideas, with pointers and suggestions for those wishing to apply these concepts to educating young people. It may also provide inspiration to explore and learn more about the events and wonders it examines.

# We need our planet for survival...

- Our relationship to the greater natural order.

- Live harmoniously with our planet.

- Sustainability.

- Interconnectedness of nature.

- Evolution of life.

- Population.

- Food.

- Soil.

- Water.

- Science: cosmology, astronomy, biology, planetary and earth sciences, physics, chemistry.

- Arts: creative disciplines.

- Nature.

- Deep time.

- Stardust to stardust.

## it does not need us

- Natural cycles on differing time scales.

- Non-anthropocentric (other-than-human) view of human race.

- Blueprint for parents, teachers, scientists and artists involved in interactive community educational projects.

- Need for outreach to all, including young children, to generate curiosity, interest, powers of observation, understanding.

- Field visits, fossils, rocks, minerals, surface processes.

- Workshops.

- Artwork.

- Talks and performances: plays, puppets.

- Museum and library visits.

- Imagination.

- Use of other resources, including people.

# StarMatter

Towards a new perspective

## Contents

# Four days over Christmas 2001

© Naomi Beth Wakan, 2001

I asked Santa (and received),

Four days relieved of social rounds,

Phone calls, and with a minimum

Of domestic chores.  The time set

Aside in order to understand physics

And the order of the Universe.

I curled up on the couch, covered

By the knitted afghan I had made

For my husband, and surrounded

By a pile of books promising

To tell me of the world before

The Big Bang, and bring me up-

To-date with news of after COBE.

I learned that Hoyle had lost

A Nobel Prize because he suggested

That flu had come from outer space,

And that Gamow just missed measuring

Cold micro-wave radiation (and a Nobel

Prize) because he was

A prankster and an alcoholic.

That Einstein smudged his record

By fudging his formulas because

He couldn't bear to admit the Universe

Might be expanding, and that Smoot

Betrayed his COBE team by jumping

The gun and letting the world

Know ahead of press-release-time

That "what we have found is

Evidence for the birth of

The Universe" but wait

That's all cosmic gossip and

I don't want to tell you that.

What I really want to let you

Know is the wonder of it all.

The wonder such as my young son

Saw in the night sky when

He demanded earnestly to know why

There were holes in it.  And

Of this wonder, I learned that,

In terms of Smarties, if one

Small red one represented our

Whole Milky Way, our Milky Way

With its $10^{11}$ stars, then the

Universe would be one kilometre

Across, but more than that,

The Universe, our Universe,

My Universe, could really be one

Gigantic black hole with all

The galaxies tucked inside.

All this has been around for

15 billion years, that's 15

With 9 zeros beside it.

So then I jotted down all the big

Numbers I was reading, such as

A nucleus being $10^{-14}$ of an atom's

Volume, and that $10^6$ atoms fit between

One serration of a postage stamp.

That gravity is $10^{-38}$ weaker than

The strong force, about which I

Have only just learned, and that

There are $10^{23}$ stars in the visible

Universe, and that the odds of life

Having started spontaneously is

1 in $10^{40,000}$, (no I didn't write

Those zeros down), but I did look

A long time at all those zeros

And tried to feel what they could mean.

I tried to pierce them with my intellect.

I tried to feel them out with my intuition,

I tried to love them with my heart.

My brain began to hurt and I wanted to

Laugh and cry at the same time.  I sensed

That if only I could tear those zeros

Apart and thrust my weary head inside

For just one moment,

I would glimpse the Gods themselves…

Not much to show for four days

Over Christmas, curled up on the couch

With my husband's striped afghan,

in the year 2001.

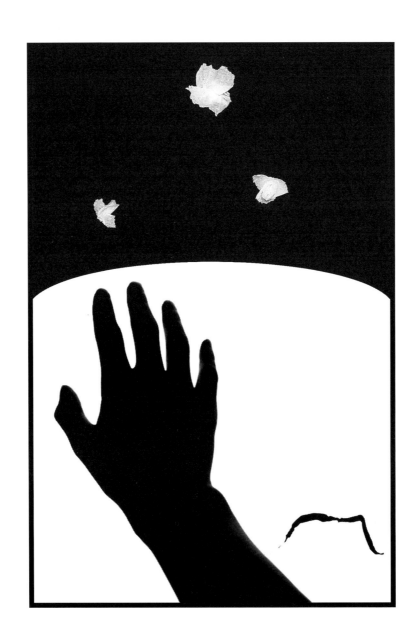

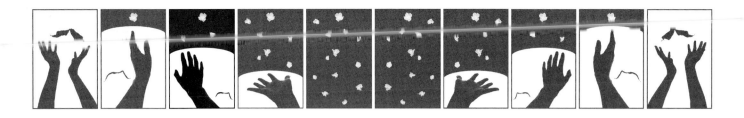

# Introduction

Leslie Brown and Tom Mason

*"Forces beyond our imagining have nudged us into shape."*

## What is StarMatter?

StarMatter is a project, which seeks ways of exploring and celebrating the world we live in, with a view to transforming our perception of our relationship to the greater natural order on which we depend, so that we can change for the better the way we live on our planet.

The project draws on both science and the arts to achieve its aims. By *'science'* we mean the areas of human endeavour, which address the origins of the universe and life – chemistry, physics, biology, and the planetary and Earth Sciences. By *'the arts'*, we mean primarily creative disciplines used for outreach education.

Humans, and particularly children, are becoming increasingly estranged from Nature through our increasingly artificial life-support systems and surroundings.

We urgently need to find ways to re-sensitize ourselves to both our interdependence with and impact on the world we live in. We believe it is only by giving our children insights into what they are and with whom they share this planet, that we can achieve a vital and long-term transformation of our relationship with the Earth.

## Where did StarMatter come from?

When we began working on StarMatter the main question was one of sustainability: how could we humans live more lightly on the planet? This expanded as our knowledge and understanding developed. Now three questions are driving this project:

❖ What meaningful outreach might help children today to understand their provenance from the Universe?

❖ How can they get a broader view of what their contributions might be; as nature to nature and as StarMatter to StarMatter?

❖ What will be the children's benefit from such a Deep Time perspective?

In the following section the story is told as to why and how these questions evolved.

## Tracing the evolution of StarMatter

The evolution of StarMatter has been a gradual one. It has spanned three years and as many continents and has progressed from a quest for sustainability to a realization that we humans are less than a blip in the history of the planet. However, a closer look at the process of developing this project reveals that its roots go back even further.

## Starting off

Avoiding the big questions of human greed, war, and whether or not man can change his nature, our first questions concerned the future of energy and related issues. We became interested in sustainability, self-sufficiency and alternative living.

To get a clearer idea of whether or not this was (or could ever be) a viable strategy, we visited many different communities in North America and Europe. Here were people who were trying to live in as self-sufficient a manner as possible – farming organically, aiming for zero waste and using solar energy. Over the months, we began to see how important it was continually to revisit and redefine sustainability, applying experience and new scientific knowledge. We saw how difficult it was to achieve the sustainable ideal – how vulnerable those farms were, how few in the world were able to practice this life style. Self-sufficiency in particular seemed to be an *'unsustainable myth'*, even though sustainability, within certain parameters, may not be.

## A kayaking adventure

During the summer of 2000, we stayed with a community on Cortes Island, off the west coast of British Columbia, Canada. Inspired by the majestic landscapes and surrounding water, members of our team decided to go kayaking. The teacher, Mike, was a marine biologist.

Under Mike's expert direction, we managed the task of getting afloat, all the time concentrating on keeping our balance. Hovering between air and water, we suddenly became conscious of our vulnerability and insignificance within nature's wider context.

Once afloat, we ventured northwards, exchanging the safe confines of accessible beaches for a more rugged shoreline of sheer rock faces, which towered above us. A bald eagle majestically circled the treetops overhead. We peered into the habitat of giant squid, fat starfish and kelp, a world, which till then had been unknown to us.

As we travelled, Mike brought up the subject of ice-core drilling, a method of accessing records of the atmosphere from the last glaciation. Ice core drilling examines tiny bubbles of ancient atmosphere trapped within the ice core. It has aided our understanding of climate change, the speed and onset of change and climatic extremes. It was the first time we had heard of this method and it instantly created for us an image of the planet not just as somewhere we humans live, but as a being with its own history and stories.

Later, Mike muttered that the world would manage perfectly well without us – it was we who needed the world in order to survive: we are part of it. Prompted by his words, we asked the question as to whether – and if so, how – humans had benefited this planet?

We glided silently over the Pacific expanses, gazing mesmerized through and over transparent waters, pondering these questions. This was the vastest expanse we had ever experienced at water level. The effect of a regular paddling rhythm, with the clear balmy air, and an occasional bird as sole distraction, induced a near-mystical state. It was hard to imagine the violent volcanic origins of this watery world. We were immersed in matters that were *other than human*.

## Sustainability and beyond

Inspired by our kayaking experience with Mike and the questions it had raised, we joined our local geological association. And to our amazement an utterly vast backdrop unfolded, one on which was perched everything else we knew, which went way beyond anything we had embraced in science to date. We had entered the world of *Deep Time*.

Deep Time is a term introduced by geology writer John McPhee. It refers to the timescale by which geologists measure life cycles of planets and rock and it is vastly different from the everyday timescale we humans live in. The Deep Time of astronomers goes back three times further.

In this context, we saw how urgent it was to broaden the domestic agrarian perspective of sustainability. We often debate the issue of organic food but, without the creation of soil, there would be no organic food in the first place. Moreover, soil itself could not have come into being without the creation of the planet Earth – or without the specific conditions that allowed Earth to form an atmosphere and acquire the life support systems that we and other species need to survive.

We saw how it is no longer enough for us to simply *do our thing*, or for our children to *do their thing*. To continue to evolve, we humans have to widen our ideas of sustainability, human existence, and life itself so that our worldview includes not only us, but also the wider biosphere of which we are part. It was around this time that we came across the work of Thomas

Berry, a theologian based in the US. Berry's vision is of an *other than human*' worldview; one which aims to counterbalance the limits of our people-based educational system.

While anthropocentrism has enabled us to do more than blink mindlessly at a sunset like an early reptile, it may also have blinded us to some realities about our relative position in the great scheme of things – realities of which we are only now becoming aware. We realized that maybe our excitement at these discoveries can provide the energy to find a less anthropocentric means of educating ourselves, and our children.

Inspired by this, we began to seek ways of exploring our world with the emphasis on the '*other than human*'.

## Into Deep Time

From a Deep Time perspective, we humans are a mere blip within the sixty-five million years that make up the Cenozoic, or '*recent life*', era. This is a far tinier blip of course, in the context of the overall timeframe of life on Earth, let alone the lifespan of the universe as a whole.

To get a picture of the magnitude of this timeframe, imagine the 4.6 billion years of Earth's lifetime represented on a 24-hour clock. The first simple cells appear at 4 a.m. At 8 p.m. multicellular life first appears on the scene and humans arrive at a few seconds before midnight.

This vast timeframe stores a rich history; a history which tells of the development of the Earth's biodiversity. By studying this history we can see how the myriad life forms, which shape our current biosphere, evolved and survived and, in many cases, died out.

Compare humanity's brief existence with some other life forms, many of which have survived for thousands of millions of years. For example, the giant tubeworms that live on the volcanic ridges of Earth's oceans survive in total darkness, and are remarkable for their ability to live indirectly on geothermal energy with no need for sunlight. Occasionally they are cremated as the underwater volcanic vents erupt around them. When local eruptions cease, juvenile worms must migrate along the ridge in search of life-giving volcanic activity and associated bacterial populations.

The tubeworms are only one example of the many simple organisms that have survived the great mass extinctions, which pepper the history of our planet. We humans should take note that while these organisms survived, more complex species died, often falling prey to changes in salinity or temperature. We must marvel at the adaptability of deep-water life forms like the tubeworms – and the simplicity of their needs.

It is thanks to many things, including the meteorite impact, which marked the end of the Cretaceous period that we mammals have flourished. We inherit the present from those who have gone before. Like Newton, we can say we are standing on the shoulders of giants; perhaps we should add the word *'worms'* too! However, unless we acknowledge and accept responsibility for our impact upon the survivability of our living companion species, we could ourselves end up being an agent of mass extinction.

## A foray into cosmology

Our explorations into matters like this naturally led us on to another question: where did our planet itself come from? And so we began to explore aspects of cosmology, the origins of our universe. Yet another realization was in store for us; that everything, including us, originates from StarMatter, the debris of dying stars. If we are four seconds on the twenty-four-hour clock of Earth's lifetime, we are far, far less than that in terms of the life of the Universe.

## The Big Bang

By now almost everyone interested in the wider world of science and the origin of humans has heard of the Big Bang. This is a convenient shorthand way of describing a defining instant in the history of our existence, not simply as humans but as creatures of the stars.

At an instant in time, less than 1 second, the entire universe was created in a monstrous explosion. Before there was nothing: some believe that this is a difficulty, and that prior to the explosion there must have been something, either a guiding hand or a master plan of the event, and so they see God. The truth is still unknown and probably unknowable, so whatever you are comfortable with is as good an explanation as any other.

The physical conditions of the Big Bang are thought to have been unusual, and part of the never-ending tussle between the cosmology theorists and the experimenters and observers is the attempt to resolve what these conditions were like. How could matter and antimatter have coexisted? Even for a moment. Is there a multitude of other parallel universes with different time streams?

## Stellar life cycles

What controls stellar life cycles? Like us, stars are born, mature and eventually die: but some end their time in a spectacular explosion, while others simply expand greatly and then contract back to eventually fizzle out like a guttering candle. In a star's birth, its future is written in its mass. The greater the mass, the shorter the life cycle. So once more we can wonder at the fact that an ordinary little star like our sun is primed for a relatively long life.

With the longsighted reach of the Hubble Space Telescope (HST) we can map out the life cycle of stars. When we observe the gaseous nebulae, like those in the Orion constellation's sword, we see enormous diffuse clouds of gas and dust, and enfolded within them are star nurseries. Partly concealed in the denser parts of the gassy zones new stars are born. As time proceeds, gravity pulls dust and gas and matter together until there is a spinning disk. As the spin rate speeds up, the temperature rises and a protostar forms. By this stage enough mass has accumulated to prime the fusion reaction that lies at the heart of every star's core. When the temperature reaches 15 million degrees centigrade, the star's nuclear furnace fires up. Radiation from the newborn stars lights up the gas clouds from within, placing them amongst the most spectacular sights in the heavens. This is a main sequence star, and it remains stable for millions or billions of years.

The star's fusion reactor compresses the simplest gas hydrogen and fuses it to make helium, giving off enormous energy in the process. As the core processes all of its hydrogen it becomes unstable and contracts, while the outer shell, which is hydrogen, cools and expands. The cooling star changes colour and becomes a red giant. All stars evolve and follow this pathway to the red giant phase. What follows next depends on the star's initial mass; basically how much matter was available in the nebular birthplace.

## Stars like our Sun

These are medium sized stars and throughout the red giant part of their lives, the hydrogen in the outer shell of the star burns and the core temperature rises. When the temperature gets to 200 million centigrade, the helium in the core fuses and forms carbon. The hydrogen gas in the outer shell blows away and forms a ring around the core. This is called a planetary nebula. When this stage in the star's life is reached, it is geriatric. The core contracts under the influence of gravity. The carbon in the core is stable and incompressible. The core remnants, typically about 20% of the original mass, collapse to form a much smaller, extremely dense body called a white dwarf. These dying stars glow white-hot and continue to do so until all of their energy has been consumed. This stage can last for millions of years until the star eventually cools to a black dwarf, essentially a cinder left over from the original star.

## Massive stars and supernovae

More massive stars than the sun have a more dramatic end, as they become unstable they form supergiants, in these huge stars the core is compressed more and more until the end product is mostly iron. At this stage no further compression and fusion is possible and the iron starts to absorb the energy. And now something dramatic occurs: in as little as a second, the core temperature rises to over a hundred billion degrees. Now the repulsive forces outweigh the force of gravity and a huge supernova explosion occurs.

The shock wave of this blast now passes through the outer layers that were being shed from the star, and this shock forms more heavy elements, including unstable radioactive isotopes. This celestial alchemy creates the raw material of the next star cycle: it also is the material from which all of us are made. We are StarMatter.

## Pulsars

If the original star was about 5 times the mass of our sun, the core remaining after the supernova becomes a neutron star. These spin quickly and emit pulses of radio waves. The rapid spin can make the radio waves sweep across the sky like the light from a lighthouse. They are then called pulsars.

## Black holes

If the original star's mass is even greater, around 10 to 15 times bigger than our Sun, the core after the supernova is still enormous. There is no fusion and so the core is consumed by its own gravity and a black hole is born. As matter is sucked into the gravity well that is the black hole, it emits X-rays from its periphery/event horizon (Hawking radiation), and this is the black hole's radiation signature.

## Accretion of matter

Why do the dust and other nebular material accrete in the first place? As things become more massive the gravitational attraction increases, and so other loose material within a given radius is drawn into the heart of the nascent star. Normally there will be a disk of dust and rock and ice that circles the star, and from this material planets are formed. They spin around the star, with the smaller heavier rocky planets condensing out closer to the star, and larger gassy planets further: they all spin in orbits that lie in the same plane. This cosy relationship of planets to their suns is even now being challenged by the discovery in the past few years of large numbers of planets that orbit stars other than the sun. None have been directly observed but their presence is inferred by some clever observational science, looking for changes in the intensity of a star's light or in interference with its steady orbit. Some massive planets spin closer to their suns than current theory predicts. So the theories, like all good science, are being rewritten. Our knowledge of these processes evolves on an almost daily basis.

It is also worth remembering that the sun also spins on its axis. This is easily observed by looking at the sun's disk through special filters to observe sunspots moving across the face of the star. One of the mysteries of our well observed sun is why the temperature of its surface is only around 6000 degrees while the sun's atmosphere, or more properly, its corona, is millions of degrees hotter.

If you look under a bed in a room that has not been used for some time you will see dust kitties.  These are aggregations of old fluff and debris that are attracted to each other, probably by electrostatic attraction.
The gregarious dust kitties accrete in a similar way to the stars and planets condensing from dust clouds in space.

When we consider our planet's accretion and study the cosmological background to the formation of the Milky Way we discover a different walk through time.  We can begin to understand the intertwining of our living human forms and the stardust that glitters in our cosmic ancestry.  We recognize an interdependency, which we have not previously appreciated.

From this cosmic perspective we can see that our ancestry is part of a constant dance; a dance that involves the creation and discharge of energies, the creation and combination of elements, the balance between these and an extremely ephemeral stability.  Even as you read this, you are influenced and bombarded by forces originating from beyond as well as within our planet.  Forces beyond our imagining have nudged us into shape and could dislodge us with little warning – transforming us, literally and metaphorically, into some other form of StarMatter.

## How to reach out

Now we had a sense of the story we wished to explore and celebrate – the story of Earth in relation to Deep Time, Deep Life and cosmology. However, we weren't yet sure of the way in which this story could be communicated.  In other words, which outreach tools would help us nurture a deeper vision of this story for coming generations, as we enter a new century with the knowledge that during the previous one we have destroyed much of our biodiversity?

We were aware of two main concerns.  Firstly, we knew that this project would need to get across some amazing insights revealed by disciplines which, up to now, have been more or less closed shops to the uninitiated (especially in the fields of astrophysics, evolutionary biology and chemistry).  Secondly, we sensed that we needed to be able not only to articulate some of these complex realities in accessible language, but also to find ways of communicating them in new ways, using the resources of contemporary arts practices.

In the year leading up to the development of this blueprint we had been exploring voice and theatre work.  Artists in our team thought that a combination of these disciplines could offer one way of communicating the vast story of our planet.

Then we met Gordon MacLellan and embarked on the 'A Life of Stone' project in 2001.  It became clear that many of the creative strategies used in that project could provide one way of inspiring and educating our children for the years and centuries to come.

But how could we combine this information and experience in a format that parents and educators, scientists and artists could understand and appreciate? The answer developed organically. We began by knowing that there was a lifetime's worth of material simply in the realm of the Earth Sciences alone. As we delved into this material, we started at the same time to explore the practical arts outreach activities we had done. More questions presented themselves, driving us to broaden our scope scientifically, creatively and practically. Over the course of six months we began to tie this material together in a form that we hope will be accessible to parents and teachers, scientists and artists. What began as a publication developed into something else: a practical blueprint for developing, through the arts and science, a greater awareness of our relationship to the natural world which supports us, in order to effect change.

## The philosophy and rationale behind this project

StarMatter has been developed as a blueprint primarily for parents, teachers, artists and scientists involved in interactive and community education projects. As the primary groups working with young people and children, parents and teachers are perhaps best placed to communicate the urgency of our current position and the need to review our relationship with our planet and Universe. StarMatter is needed for a number of reasons.

❖ As mentioned earlier, it is vital for our physical, psychological and spiritual survival that we, particularly our children, succeed in re-sensitizing ourselves to our place in the natural order – and that we can be moved to discover ways of transforming our relationship with our planet.

❖ What this project offers is a strict adherence to holistic science together with a firm link to the creative arts. We believe this bridging exercise is akin to offering different lenses other than the ones predominantly worn by mankind.

❖ Glasses that will offer a deeper vision of nature and allow us better to appraise our place as merely one strand within the web of nature.

❖ Through our projects, we wish to encourage a greater cosmological rather than material perception and value system, and to illustrate that yes, even six-year-old children can be touched by and interpret in their own way such complex matters. Ultimately we hope this will help promote a sense of the miraculous, and a wish to embrace a more holistic perspective with a view to change.

❖ StarMatter also encourages innovation, both creatively and scientifically.

❖ Our projects should have at their heart a willingness to explore new artistic forms and languages. They should also be willing to absorb the latest strands in scientific thinking – without sacrificing accuracy or thoroughness in research.

❖ Developing StarMatter projects will entail a necessary download of a large amount of scientific data.  In our blueprint we have summarized areas and sources of research, which we believe that teachers, parents, artists, scientists and above all, children can and will find useful.

We hope this project will make a difference.  We hope that it will motivate others to continue exploring the story of our planet and universe.  More urgently than this, we hope it will encourage people to keep communicating that story to the children of our world so that they might make a difference.

Ultimately, we hope StarMatter will inspire others as we have been inspired by our past and present teachers, to whom we offer much thanks.

# Before

Before everything

Before anything... at all

A quiet Voice spoke

And from nowhere Darkness awoke.

*Extract from class poem by pupils
of the Wesley Methodist Primary School,
Buxton, Derbyshire, UK.*

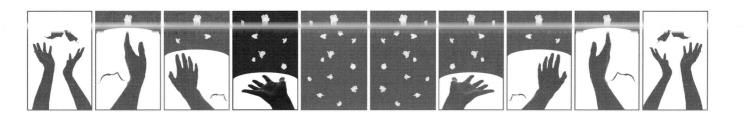

# Arts, Science and the need for outreach

Tom Mason and Chris Vis

## How science is communicated

Over the last two to three hundred years, science has become an increasingly specialized subject. Individual fields of discovery and exploration are growing ever further apart, with the result that individual scientists – let alone the layperson – often have difficulties understanding areas beyond their scope of study. Factors such as the specialized language used by the different scientific disciplines, the constantly changing nature of scientific enquiry and the detailed nature of scientific research do not help this situation.

To an extent this has been addressed by the emergence of popular science books exploring key areas. However, in the main, these books are targeted at adults, and can involve a degree of *'dumbing down'* which flattens the subject matter and smoothes out interesting inconsistencies.

While progress has been made in developing scientific outreach projects – aimed at presenting and exploring key concepts and research areas to young people in a meaningful way – there is still a sense that something is missing in the way we learn and explore science concepts. Most importantly is a sense of a gap between scientific facts as they are discovered and their relevance to us as holistic human beings who operate on physical, mental and spiritual levels. As human beings, scientists are no different from any other person. Many may have a spiritual dimension to their lives that suggests our existence has a purpose beyond everyday awareness – a purpose that through the centuries has been defined by the various religions. Scientific and religious insights can be reconcilable, as long as it is realized that they are totally different categories of the human experience.

We believe it is important to explore scientific research areas accurately, in detail and to a high level of complexity – while at the same time highlighting the material, psychological and spiritual relevance of these areas. Let us take geology as an example which, as it concerns itself with the history and evolution of the planet we live on, is central to any study of the Earth Sciences. We all live on this planet, and owe it to ourselves to understand as best we can how it works. Yet how many of us truly appreciate the uniqueness of our planet?  The *'Goldilocks'* hypothesis says that the Earth is uniquely placed in the cosmic dance around the Sun. Not too hot like Venus, nor too cold like Mars: the Earth's orbit, like the porridge Goldilocks eventually eats, is just right.  Its position allows the Earth to be three-quarters covered by the oceans of liquid water that sustain all life on the planet.

Our large solitary Moon is also different to those orbiting other planets. In fact, without the oceans sloshing around the Earth's shorelines under the influence of the Moon's gravitational field, we would likely not be here. We know that early vertebrates first evolved in the shallow seas and estuaries of the Earth's tidally influenced coastlines.

From geological research, we are now aware that humanity's position in the web of life on Earth may be explained by the statistics of evolution taking place in a very long time span: what we later refer to as Deep Time. The fossil record indicates that life appeared on Earth very early, suggesting that life, wherever it takes root, is extremely tenacious.

These discoveries have implications for us not just in terms of scientific fact, but in relation to our very perception of ourselves in relation to the planet we live on and with.

## Building bridges: the role of the arts in education

We believe it is not enough simply to present scientific facts in a dry and technical way.  In order for young people in particular to become aware of the relevance of these facts and relationships, we must find another way in. For this reason, we have placed a lot of emphasis on the use of the arts to explore, integrate and communicate areas of scientific research.

During the latter half of the twentieth century, much has been written about the importance of art in education.  There also seems to be a growing appreciation of the role of the arts in the curriculum of primary and secondary schools.  However, school authorities and parents alike often misunderstand the role of the arts in education.

Often art is regarded as a subject in its own right, to be treated quite separately from any other subject.  By many it is seen as a *'relaxing'* subject, giving the pupil a chance to *'unwind'*; it teaches them a hobby which might come in useful in later life, and yes, if a student shows a more than average amount of talent, he or she could pursue it as a career.  In many instances, colleges have used art as useful *'remedial'* classes, on which *'difficult'* pupils can be offloaded.

## Why we need an *'aesthetic education'*

While it may be hard to disagree with some of the above sentiments, most writers on art education see the role of the arts as a means through which to educate in a far broader sense than is normally perceived.

To quote, for example, Herbert Read:

*"The purpose of education can only be to develop, at the same time as the uniqueness, the social consciousness or reciprocity of the individual. As a result of the infinite permutations of heredity, the individual will inevitably be unique, and this uniqueness, because it is something not possessed by anyone else, will be of value to the community. It may be only a unique way of speaking or of smiling – but that contributes to life's variety. But it may be a unique way of seeing, of thinking, of expressing mind or emotion – and in that case, one man's individuality may be of incalculable benefit to the whole of humanity. But uniqueness has no practical value in isolation. One of the most certain lessons of modern psychology and of recent historical experience, is that education must be a process, not only individuation, but also of integration, which in the reconciliation of individual uniqueness with social unity. From this point of view, the individual will be 'good' to the degree that his individuality is realized within the organic wholeness of the community. His touch of colour contributes, however imperceptibly, to the beauty of the landscape – his note is a necessary, though unnoticed, element in the universal harmony."*
(Read, *'Education through Art.'* Faber & Faber, 1944.)

Read talks more specifically about the arts as much as art as a means of education:

*"It must be understood from the beginning that what I have in mind is not merely 'art education' as such, which should more properly be called visual or plastic education: the theory to be put forward embraces all modes of self-expression, literary and poetic (verbal) no less than musical or aural, and forms an integral approach to reality which should be called aesthetic education – the education of those senses upon which consciousness, and ultimately the intelligence and judgement of the human individual, are based. It is only insofar as these senses are brought into harmonious and habitual relationship with the external world that an integrated personality is built up. Without such integration we get, not only the psychologically unbalanced types familiar to the psychiatrist, but what is even more disastrous from the point of view of the general good, those arbitrary systems of thought, dogmatic or rationalistic in origin, which seek in despite of the natural facts to impose a logical or intellectual pattern on the world of organic life."*
(Read, *'Education through Art.'* Faber & Faber, 1944.)

From this we can see the emphasis Read places upon the arts and the incompleteness of education without them. We may assume he would have had no difficulty in including dance, mime and other performance within this all-embracing approach.

How near are we to this goal?

We saw in the previous section that science is a creative activity. However is science in any way being taught as a creative activity? In StarMatter we are hoping to bring together left brain and right brain approaches so that the young person can develop a greater awareness and sensitivity to their place in the great tapestry that is life on Earth.

Let us first have a look at what left brain and right brain approaches are. According to Jerre Levy, in 'Psychological Implications of Bilateral Asymmetry',

"...the left hemisphere (brain) analyses over time, whereas the right hemisphere synthesizes over space".

A complete education, as advocated by Read and as proposed in this blueprint by StarMatter, would develop both sides of the brain. The authors of this document have noticed on more than one occasion that students who had difficulties in learning subjects involving rational, objective and analytic thinking activities associated with the left brain improved remarkably when they were able to develop the right side of the brain – the dreamer, the artist, the intuitionist.

However, it seems reasonable to conclude that in most of our schools Read's ideal form of education – education through art – is far from being implemented to the extent that he proposed.

## Neglecting the right brain

In our present-day school system, the right brain goes largely untaught. Most schools do teach art, creative writing and perhaps courses in music. But we rarely find courses in imagination, visualization, in perceptual or spatial skills, in inventiveness, in intuition, in creativity as a separate subject.

Educators who apparently value these skills seem to think that students will develop them as a 'natural' consequence of training in verbal, analytical skills. That such development often does occur in spite of the school system is surely a proof of the survival capacity of the right brain, rather than an indication of the effectiveness of such an approach.

Unfortunately, our culture has emphasized so strongly the development of left brain skills that our students lose a large proportion of the potential ability of the other half of their brain. The effects of inadequate training in verbal or computational skills are only too well known. The left brain finds it hard to fully recover, and the effects may handicap students for life. One wonders what happens to the right brain, which is hardly trained at all!

"By the time the child can draw more than a scribble, by age three or four years, an already well-formed body of conceptual knowledge formulated in language dominates his memory and controls his graphic

*work… Drawings are graphic accounts of essentially verbal processes. As an essentially verbal education gains control, the child abandons his graphic efforts and relies almost entirely on words. Language has first spoilt drawing and then swallowed it up completely."*
(Karl Buhler, 1930.)

## Where to go from here?

Let us hope, now that neuroscientists have provided a conceptual base for right brain training, that educators may begin to build a school system that will train the whole brain. The effects of this could be truly revolutionary. As Betty Edwards (1992), author of *'Drawing on the Right Side of the Brain'*, Souvenir Press, has written:

*"A creative person is one who can process in new ways the information directly at hand - the ordinary sensory data available to all of us. A writer needs words, a musician needs notes, an artist needs visual perceptions, and all need some knowledge of the techniques of their crafts. But a creative individual intuitively sees possibilities of transforming ordinary data into a new creation, transcendent over the mere raw materials."*

Observation is a skill which would be very much part and parcel of this kind of creative education.

*"Learning to draw is really a matter of learning to see – to see correctly – and that means a good deal more than merely looking with the eye."*
(Kimon Nicolaides, 1941, *'The Natural Way to Draw.'* Andre Deutsch.)

*"Unless we penetrate into an experience whatever its nature may be, it will remain superficial and cannot serve as a basis for creativity."*
(Victor Lowenfeld, 1969, *'The Creative and Mental Growth of the Child.'* Macmillan.)

As many have written, the skill of observation goes beyond the physical act of seeing. It has profound psychological implications for our understanding ourselves as individuals and as elements in a far greater picture.

*"The development of an Observer can allow a person considerable access to observing different identity states, and an outside observer may often clearly infer different identity states, but a person himself who has not developed the Observer function very well may never notice the many transitions from one identity state to another."*
(Charles T. Tart, 1975, *'Alternative States of Consciousness.'* E.P. Dutton.)

## A positive role-model

In previous centuries, artists and scientists were not put into separate boxes the way they are today. Leonardo da Vinci (1452–1519) was one person who saw no contradiction in being an artist, an inventor and a scientist.

Reading his notebooks, one notices a man with a boundless curiosity. He explored painting techniques and hydraulic engineering, comparative anatomy and musical instruments, massive sculpture and all kinds of machines.

> *"There is no antagonism in Leonardo's mind between art and science."*

(Anna Maria Brizio, 1981, *"The words of Leonardo"* in *'Leonardo, the Scientist.'* Hutchinson.)

There is probably no better way to conclude this section than with some thoughts from Leonardo himself. These will give you a sense of the breadth of Leonardo's curiosity and the way in which he approached his vast range of subjects.

> *"... it is my intention first to cite experience, then to demonstrate through reasoning why experience must operate in a given way."* (MS, E 55r.)

> *"No part of the Earth exposes itself by the depredations of the course of the waters which was not once a land surface seen by the sun."* (Atlanticus, 45V-A.)

> *"If you disparage painting, which alone imitates all the visible works of nature, you disparage a most subtle science which by philosophical reasoning examines all kinds of forms; on land and in the air, plants, animals, grass and flowers, which are all bathed in shadow and light. Doubtless this science is the true daughter of nature..."* (MS, A 100r.)

## Scientific outreach

So far we have outlined the need for scientific research to be accurate and detailed. We have also emphasized the need for us as human beings to begin to integrate the two different sides of our brain so that we can learn more fully and in a more self-realized way.

As outreach is a key element in the StarMatter blueprint, let us now take a look at scientific outreach; what it is, how it has been – and is being – carried out and the benefits it can bring to a non-scientific audience.

Outreach is the process by which a professional scientist uses their storytelling skills to *'show and tell'*, thereby personalizing the teaching experience for the learner. Apart from a comfortable familiarity with the subject, outreach needs no special skills other than a huge infectious enthusiasm for the topic – and, of course, the ability to spin a good yarn! In the case of young audiences, it is easy to tell stories that the children already know and to weave new information into this familiar context.

## The power of curiosity

One essential human quality is our innate curiosity. For a seminar in *'smart learning'*, watch any young person explore their surroundings by touch, taste and smell. Even when we are older and ostensibly more *civilized*, we still instinctively learn in the same way. The smart outreach leader will exploit this curiosity as a matter of course – in fact, this is the whole reason for outreach activities in the first place.

We have a visceral need to understand and to see for ourselves: the *'Doubting Thomas'* syndrome. This is the kernel reason for doing teaching of any kind, and is it is especially important when doing outreach to realize that we continue to need these personal stimuli for efficient learning.

Besides curiosity, another defining human characteristic is our ability to think about things in the abstract. However, to do this well, we already must have practiced and assimilated the repertoire of experience that we need to process the abstract thoughts. When we were small, we all learnt how to write when we got our hands on the tools: practice made us perfect. Just as there is no substitute for the actual writing experience, so there is no better way to teach people about geology than by showing them, and allowing them to get their hands on the specimens. It is always easier to explain when you are on site, or when you bring the specimens to the students.

## Demonstration and observation

For example, if we want to demonstrate the complexity and continuity of the web of life on Earth, what better way to start than in a quarry full of fossils? Almost everywhere on the planet is within reach of some place where fossils are abundant. Careful inspection will yield fossils that add up to an ancient community, maybe a fossil coral reef. Everyone has seen modern reefs and their creatures on television or film, so they already have visual images in their memory.

Now the mentor needs to fill in the gaps and join the dots: painting word pictures of the sedentary corals, their lifestyles dependent on their algal symbionts; their predators and the multitude of other organisms that shared their time and space. The mentor's arms will describe fighter pilot arcs as they talk of the water depth, patrolled by spiny sharks. Blank note pages can be filled with sketches and drawings, images can be made in the mud and sand of the quarry floor. Use whatever comes to hand to emphasize dynamically the three-dimensional reality of these long dead animals.

The mentor can then lead onto deductions: if these fossils are corals then the water was possibly warm, dappled with sunlight, noisy with the sound of the ocean. Recent discoveries of deep cold-water corals living in darkness have changed the traditional view that all corals live in warm shallow water. To support the building complexity the scientist can mention other types of fish, maybe not found at this site, but known from elsewhere. Learners may bring rare fossils that are diagnostic of a very specific time, allied to the planktonic drifters, the scavengers and the crawlers, all building up into a complete ecosystem of the mind.  Of course amateurs will bring crystals and other eye catching inorganic things which aren't fossils, even modern bird poop mistaken for bone, but that aids the digestion of this rich seam of learning.  The mistakes are the roughage.

## Building a picture

For the beginning scientist, and even for the adult learner, the realization that the tiny organic fragments that they have found for themselves are the shells and skeletons of long dead animals is truly mind-expanding.  It is a humbling experience for anyone, as the synapses click and the brain makes the connections.  The leap of imagination, the amazing human ability to visualize and conceptualize the what, where and when of this organism: this is what makes scientists tick.  This is the experience that Howard Carter had when he first saw the riches of the boy pharaoh Tutankhamun.  By taking students to a field site, the scientist is providing the gift of ownership.

These fossils are things that the learners have been able to find for themselves.  Yes, the expert teacher or mentor has now put them in context, but the experience is all theirs.  One of the sublime pleasures of teaching is that moment when you see the light dawning in your students' eyes, after all of the explanations, all the arm waving, the sifting of the evidence in front of them for this ancient landscape, now they know, just like you.  They can read the rocks.  It is the Damascene moment, when the acquisition of the knowledge is added to the bedrock of the more important understanding.

## How has most geological outreach been carried out?

Most geological outreach takes place on field trips when visitors are taken to sites where rock-forming processes may be shown, such as ancient volcanic terrains, or, as described above, where specific fossils can be collected to explain how an ancient environment functioned.  Most countries have easily accessible sites, which can be shown to the casual visitor without great danger.  This can be an expensive way of starting out, and most outreach commences with a series of talks at universities with associated practical sessions in the laboratories.  This allows beginners to find their feet and also to get a feel for the subject.  It also means that they can decide whether they are comfortable with the teacher's personality and style as this will be a very important relationship.  The learner must feel that they can talk to their mentor, while the mentor must be open and approachable to make the learning experience fun.  The learner ought to come away from sessions fired with the need to know more.

## An outreach example

In the southern continents, there are many important sites that document how life evolved on land. These animals are especially abundant in the huge area of semi-desert Karoo landscape in South Africa.

One of the authors of this document was involved in working on these sites with a group of amateur palaeontologists. After sessions in the classroom, he planned a weekend family-friendly field trip to show the group the sites. These included places where fossil plants, mostly *Glossopteris* leaves, could be collected, as well as a small hill that was studded with the fossil remains of small herbivorous mammal-like reptiles, and rarer remains of their predators and other animals of the environment.

The rocks told a story of flat flood plains, with meandering streams, and ephemeral lakes. The lake shallows were often beautifully preserved with their sandstone surfaces sculpted by ripple marks that were enlivened by clear footprint trails made by these long dead animals. The group could see where their tails had dragged in the mud and sand, where the sand had been semi-liquid and splashed as they walked across it. Small worms and larvae, whose modern relatives still behave in the same way, produced hieroglyphic squiggles in the finer muddy layers.

There were abundant skulls and vertebrae, tiny toe bones, and broad scapulae, and the very distinctive tusk-shaped teeth of the Lystrosaurus who lived in these places 250 million years before we arrived on the scene. The people on the field trip found whole skeletons, loose jaws, skulls, ribs and tusks: in fact a small herd of *Lystrosaurus* could have been assembled from the finds.

It was hot and dusty, it was thirsty work, but as the sun set over the green hills of Natal that evening, the group went back to the campsite for a barbecue and cold beers. The mentor showed them slides and how their fossils finds could be reconstructed. The group picked the loose flakes of clay from the skulls, and blew dust off the fossil leaves. They talked about the lungfish burrows that they found, and the small D-shaped amphibian skulls with complicated patterns inscribed on the bone. In the words of this author, *"I bet that the experience of that weekend will colour their dinner party conversations and their interpretation of their personal landscapes until they die. That is why I do outreach."*

## Looking to the future

It is always difficult to be a soothsayer, but one essential future change must involve the blurring of the science – arts interface. This was always an artificial divide, fostered by the divisions that we impose on our school children's tightly packed curriculum. With a modicum of enlightened thinking and a willingness to think outside the strictures of the school curriculum, we can easily change this.

A talk on dinosaurs to a class of primary children can be extended into an art class by making collage images of the popular dinosaurs, or by making clay models of the animals and their environment. An artificial volcano, made with fizzy chemicals, food colouring and water can extend the imagination and lead to creative writing sessions, plays and poems.

This is the way that teaching used to be when there was time for teachers to constructively digress to satisfy children's juvenile curiosity and their probing questions. If we need to do this now through outreach visits with external experts, let us insist that these outreach activities be a normal, curriculum-broadening part of the school week, rather than a special or occasional diversion.

## Outreach and the arts

In the past when science was in its infancy, few saw anything unusual in a person being well acquainted with the arts and the sciences. This is the image of the Renaissance scholar, epitomized by Leonardo da Vinci, a character familiar with the full breadth of human knowledge. While it may be a bigger task now to fully appreciate the enormous vista of our knowledge base, it surely is worth striving to ensure that people are aware of this so that it becomes the norm in the future. There is huge opportunity for personal artistic inspiration from a knowledge and understanding of science.

It is surely no surprise that the genre of science fiction is so popular, and that people are enthralled by the futuristic vision of humanity in space. In a way we are returning to our origins, for of course we are all children of the stars. Our very substance, the atoms of our bones and sinews, were created in the fusion furnace heart of a star. When the ageing star eventually blew apart in a supernova explosion, the elements of its death became the building bricks of our Solar System, and ultimately of ourselves. This is poetry, religion, mysticism and art wrapped up in incontrovertible scientific fact.

Fire rocks give form to the land,

And rain washes them clean in the sea.

Rolled and crushed and swept by time,

Forged gems in the depths of the ground.

*Extract from class poem by pupils
of the Wesley Methodist Primary School,
Buxton, Derbyshire, UK.*

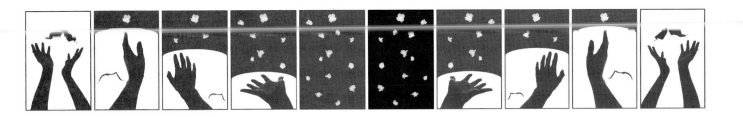

# Science and Creativity

Gordon MacLellan

*Before*
*Before everything*
*Before anything... at all*
*A quiet Voice spoke*
*And from nowhere Darkness awoke.*

This and all the other poetry quotations in this section are from a poem written by the children of the Wesley Methodist Primary School involved in the Drama stream of this case study. The title of the poem is 'A Life of Stone'.

This is a case study of a pilot project, which explored how Deep Time and related issues could be brought to life in a creative educational outreach context.

The project concentrated on a creative approach in the understanding that art and science working together can achieve more than either can on its own. We hope that it will inspire further creative strategies towards outreach in these and other areas.

## About Creeping Toad

Throughout this section, *'we'* refers to *'Creeping Toad'*. Creeping Toad is an environmental arts group that aims to work with groups of people to find ways of celebrating the relationships between people, wildlife and places. Toad projects mostly centre upon the work of Gordon MacLellan, a zoologist, dancer and storyteller, who was joined in *'A Life of Stone'* by Lesley Martin, a countryside ranger, designer and dramatist.

Toad projects work across a range of art forms and involve processions, giant books, puppet plays and dance pieces. We have worked with many different types of community groups, including pre-school groups, all the way through formal education, summer play schemes, family events and adult workshops. Recently our projects have taken us to the USA, South Africa and Slovakia.

Toad workshops evolve organically, operating within a general framework of art form and subject but growing and changing with the group. The work consequently can be rather unpredictable – but the effectiveness of the approach is reflected in the enthusiasm of participants and the delight of children who often return for more!

## Starting points

How do you take concepts like *'Deep Time'* and *'planetary geology'* and turn them into something that is relevant to young people, something that children can understand and explore for themselves?

From the outset, we did not want simply to plan a set of formal *'this is what you ought to know'* lessons. We felt that giving people the opportunity to explore for themselves was important. Equally important were creativity and the freedom to interpret ideas through art. This meant we were looking for a project structure that would allow young people to investigate on their own behalf, with some degree of freedom to express their discoveries.

It would have been relatively easy to design a project where children were taught things, told the facts, led through activities which are still predetermined, even though their specific learning outcomes may be concealed. But more than just *'knowing things'*, we were looking for an emotional and creative response: an interpretation of information and experience rather than a straightforward illustration of information that was already recorded.

Would this be easy to achieve, while at the same time allowing us to go into the subject matter in great depth? The simple answer was *'probably not'*. We felt that, rather than plunging into the intricacies of Deep Time and planetary geology, we needed to step back and start at an earlier stage in a journey that might, eventually, take the travellers on to such concepts. For this reason we turned to more *'Earthly'* geology and the concept of geological timescales. We also needed to present teachers with a project that looked interesting and – while perhaps not tying in directly with set curriculum targets – offered something educationally valuable within time requirements that would not disrupt other work too much. Out of this brew of hopes, ambitions and practical considerations came the first *'Life of Stone'* school workshops.

## Aims

Within these workshops we hoped to combine knowledge and creative outcomes by:

❖ Introducing students to some basic geological processes and familiarizing them with a range of rock types and human uses of stone.

❖ Encouraging an appreciation of the history of the Earth in the context of geological terms and timescales.

❖ Fostering participants' confidence within themselves as imaginative, artistic people, able to see the creative possibilities of scientific disciplines and ready to engage with and enjoy such disciplines.

These were the more straightforward aims. Others have been harder to define and do not lend themselves to easy statements.

This work would, we hoped, encourage people to step away from an anthropocentric view of the world. We wanted people to see Earth as more than just the place where people live – instead, as a world full of dynamic exciting processes worthy of exploration for their own sakes.

Reasoning that children would be familiar with descriptions of life cycles in themselves, other animals and plants, we decided to use those terms in our work with stone, in the hope that they would see geological processes as cycles where stones live out their lives. This (we hoped!) would allow us to tell the stories of stones, of rocks, which experience their own adventures but operate on timescales that are so slow that we small humans are unlikely to ever notice them happening.

## Method

It was possible, we agreed, to realize these aims. Now the question was of how and when. We decided to use an approach that would combine geology fieldwork and research with art workshops, building up towards a finale where the work of different classes would combine in a single performance.

We were, however, planning for January 2002 – and the thought of field work in the rain and cold wind sent us to Manchester University Museum's Education Department instead! Our plan was that each class would have a half-day session at the Museum, with a workshop led by Museum staff and a visit to either the rocks and minerals gallery or the fossil gallery as appropriate. This would be followed by a series of arts workshops back in school, the number of workshops varying according to the different themes that classes were set to explore. Most of the art work would centre on performance, using movement, puppets, and stories to keep the idea of action going, to keep that thought of constant change, of life cycles unfolding, active – rather than frozen into a moment of paint or sculpture.

## The school

Creeping Toad had previously worked with Wesley Methodist Primary School in Radcliffe in north Manchester and thought they would enjoy the challenge! Our previous work had shown the school to be creative and adventurous, with a real sense of education for pupils.

To their immense credit, they said *'Yes'* and the class teachers involved remained a stalwart support and invaluable sounding board as the workshops developed.

The three oldest classes all participated, amounting to about one hundred children from Years 4 to 6 (9 - 12 years of age).

## Hopes and lingering doubts

So far, we knew what we hoped to achieve, we had a school to work with and we even knew more or less how we would get from beginning to end. Even so, we entered the workshop phase with a number of concerns:

❖ Could we actually take hold of a sense of *'Deep Time'*; of time running back beyond our experience – or maybe even imagination – and make it relevant to children?

❖ How were we going to balance the relationship between the need to deliver information and the freedom to express and experiment?
It would be very easy to be caught by a need to be geologically exact, but we were determined to avoid the *'that's wrong'* approach to either geology or art.

❖ Would *'stone'* capture the children's imaginations at all?

With these doubts hovering around us, we still trusted in the people we would work with, having the confidence built over years of experience that, if we can fire imaginations, people can do just about anything. We trust our groups and know that they can achieve the things that seem impossible: we knew mountains could dance and sandstorms blow. Our work is hinged upon that belief in people and we hoped that, in the end, if this project did nothing else, it would release in its participants an excitement for and about stone.

## The Workshops

We had three classes, each working with one of three themes:

❖ Geological processes: hopefully leading to a dance/drama piece.

❖ Diversity of rocks and minerals: perhaps giving us puppets.

❖ Fossils: a visual arts strand, giving us banners to provide a backdrop for the other pieces in the final performance.

Outlines of the work of the three groups follow, mostly using extracts from our workshop journal to follow the ups and downs of the process.

## Stories

We began with stories. Gathering the three classes together for an hour of weaving tales, we woke rocks in our imaginations with tales of:

- Stones as parts of living landscape (the Icelandic troll who returns to stone in sunlight).
- The Earth as a single giant form (a creation story from China).
- Stones as sources of wonder and enchantment (a story from Scotland).
- Stones as stones, with the recurring theme of *"the stone you hold in your hand is probably older than the mountains behind you"*.

The storytelling worked well. It fired the groups up and had people talking about *'their stones'*: pebbles found on holiday, stones in gardens, parks and playgrounds, fossils bought in shops. People brought stones in to show us: small fossils, fragments of pyrites, a stone with a star cracked into it.

However, soon after this we went to the Museum to look at stones as scientists and investigators. In retrospect, we probably should have spent more time sliding one way of seeing into another. The shift might have been too abrupt: people wanted to tell adventures about their stones and were not that worried about bringing in the detail offered by museum experiences. I suppose the question is: Did we want dreams or facts?

## Museum sessions

For the drama and puppet groups, the activities held at Manchester Museum and led by the museum staff mostly centred upon identifying different rocks and getting some idea of their origins, features, age, use and so on.

Our visits to the Geology galleries proved very exciting with lots of drawing coming out of the experience. The downside here was perhaps the time available: we only had about 1.5 hours. In retrospect we could have done with more time to get more deeply into age and timescales.

## Drama

With this group we had three days to work together before final rehearsals. In a journey from Museum to story, we experimented with movement – making ourselves into mountains, erupting volcanoes, caves and stalactites. We added cloth, working co-operatively to build mountain ranges, lava flows, rivers and glaciers.

Shadow puppets flickered in as well: giving us images of evolving animal life as brief flashes in the long slow life of our stones. And it all got a bit carried away really!

## Extracts from workshop journal

### Session 1

A good start, building stories about rocks we had seen at the Museum or the stones people had brought in from home. First movement work had us building mountain ranges, volcanoes, glaciers and boulders with faces out of people.

*Performance:* looks like it will use body sculptures and cloth for geological features and maybe shadow puppets for the animals and plants that come and go through the stone's life...

Session 2

Really!  You leave these people for a week and things unfold like flowers in the sunshine!  On our return this morning, there was a display outside the drama group's classroom of all their short stories about their own stones.  There was a lovely story collage, a sequence of stories being reduced on the photocopier, down and down, compressing the stories like grains of sand, until the whole collection (30 plus stories on A6 postcards) could be fitted onto a single pebble to give the class a story stone...

There was a mountain of stories capped by words lifted from one child: *"rocks are made from crumbling mountains, mountains are made from crumbling rocks"*...  Then there was even a collective poem, a beautiful piece capturing essence of their experience of our work and their own thoughts.

So we revised to-day's workshops as we went: it seemed grossly insulting to reject their poem and try to do a new piece of collective writing of our own, so we have worked with their poem and will add more detail as we go.  We have tried to work around the idea of rocks as life forms with their own life cycle, holding onto that idea of constant change, that nothing stays the same, that rocks, grow and change all the time, only slowly... Interesting issue:  Working through the poem we were reminded that this is a church school.  Very nicely done but it is clear that their interpretation of what is going on is a Christian one... not that this is a problem, it was just a perspective that Lesley and I needed to remind ourselves of: that for our group it is God who drives the processes we are exploring.

It was good to see this, to remind ourselves that while we may be working along a science/art agenda, the people we work with will see things through their own understanding of things and that we need to respect that: that education which proscribes the outcome and does not allow for individual perspective is propaganda and not education.

Session 3

Much more of a struggle... moving on from our work with poems, movement and shadow puppets from the week before.  Movement bogged down during the morning... manipulating large pieces of cloth was proving difficult and groups were restless and competitive... felt we all were losing the passion of it.

End of morning Pete Johnstone (the teacher), Lesley and I had a good conversation, with Pete speaking as an observer and providing very useful feedback: class are struggling and getting fed up, how about giving individuals their own pieces of cloth?

Tried that after lunch: much smoother run now. However, we had a feeling that Pete, a drama person himself, was very uncertain about our very organic responsive way of working: think he is used to working with scripts telling people what to do and having them do it and our freeform evolution of things was unsettling for him.

Relationships (are) however still cheerful and supportive.

Shadow puppet sessions went well: familiar difficulty in getting children to draw large. Ideas for the explosive beginning of things, meteors on poles, *'poi'* (the whirling balls on ropes that fire-jugglers use) to give us flaming suns. Late morning and afternoon we worked on shadow puppets, intending to use these to add detail to our performance: using people we will build big things and work on large images. We felt that we could use a shadow-puppet screen like a TV set to show life forms at different times, like flickering, fleeting images against the slow-turning endurance of our stone-cycles.

Now we have *'early seas'*, dinosaurs and winged pterosaurs. Still to come: big mammals and maybe a city.

L and I ended day feeling drained, wondering how it would go next. A reminder of how vulnerable we are within this way of working: we are not detached from process at all. While we hold a long term vision and hope and maintain confidence in the group, as they go up and down we are battered by those storms ourselves and end up feeling like damp cloths well wrung out.


## Puppets

*Fire rocks give form to the land,*
*And rain washes them clean in the sea.*
*Rolled and crushed and swept by time,*
*Forged gems in the depths of the ground.*


We had two days with this group, galloping around in all directions, as we took our detailed information from museum visits and turned it into characters and the characters into puppets, most standing almost the same height as the puppeteers.

Everything grew from stones: colours, forms and behaviour (coal people scared of fire, a marble princess who wanted to be polished, and inadequately villainous sandstones who were tricked into sitting out in the rain until they eroded).  Imaginations got a bit carried away and at times it felt as if the stones themselves were being lost in the distance.  Having sample collections beside us as we worked and simple information on our stones might have helped.

A story grew nonetheless: a good old fashioned tale with a noble king (Boulder), his beautiful queen Calcite, ('*The Snake Queen*', a tough character who bit the villains and called her mountains to wake every pebble to open its eyes), a villainous lump of coal and a dodgy bit of sulphur, with their various henchmen.

In a simple tale of world domination, everything still had to be stone-based: insults, tricks, rescuing princesses, it all had to come from the stones.  And it did – making for a strange story, but a delightful one too, executed with much conviction.

## Extracts from workshop journal

### Session 2

After the trying times of the previous day, our stone people group went wild and puppets galloped towards completion as we finished heads and added bodies and limbs...

Towards the end of the day, we sat down and collectively wrote an adventure that these assorted stones might have had.  What resulted was a bizarre mix of human fairy tale – beautiful princesses, villains, noble (if boulder-lumpy) kings and heroic friends – and geology.  The settings, characters, reactions and solutions were geological ones; defeat sandstone villains by tricking them to stand in pouring rain while they erode, rescue the princess with a volcanic bomb erupting from the heart of a volcano, defeat a villainous lump of coal by heating it up.

We had originally planned to slide puppet pieces into the main dance drama but now that felt risky.  If we broke the flow of that piece and the concentration of the drama group, we could risk the wholeness of the piece.  Moreover, the puppet class seemed so together and clear about real characters within their stone people that it seemed unfair not to use them in a story form.

## Samples of *'stone insults'* from puppet story

*You are so hopeless you could not fall off a cliff if we pushed you!*

*You are so hopeless you could not start an avalanche if you fell off a mountain!*

*You are so hopeless you could not break a window if we threw you at it!*

*You are so hopeless you could not trip someone up if they stepped on you!*
*You have lived a million years and still can't squash a fly if you fall on top of it.*

## Fossils

*Breath from the Voice touches dust*
*And life rises slowly out from the sea*
*Great monsters and creatures*
*Crawl out on dry land,*
*Some take to the air with their wings.*

Two days with this group took us from close contact with fossils in the Museum, through banner design to capture the fossil that we saw and the animal or plant and environment it came from, to final preparation and construction of the banners.

A range of sizes was produced. The biggest (3m x 1m) formed a backdrop for the puppet and dance pieces, while the others were paraded on poles and then set around the hall to surround the audience with images of life and stones. This most straightforward of workshops gave very colourful and dramatic results, with great care going into the planning and production of the banners. We worked with masking tape and fabric paint, blanking out images with tape and adding colour everywhere else. This gives very bold final results and is an easy technique for individuals to take on board and use themselves elsewhere.

## Extracts from workshop journal

Lovely museum session on Monday. Working in a different classroom than previously: smaller but brighter and more comfortable space.

Group split to spend time on hands-on fossil work with Museum education staff: looking at how fossils are made, rocks you find them in, age and handling specimens, recording with drawing and rubbings. The other group went with me to the Fossil gallery where we looked at the animals that might have been and made drawings of animals and plants.

Encouraging people to look at smaller animals, fish, Cambrian life forms and plants as well as the beautifully made and very dramatic marine reptiles and dinosaurs...

Also visited Museum's aquarium to look at possible habitats and see tree frog tadpoles in a wonderful swamp setting, reminding us of all the animals and plants that may never have fossilized.

Very successful session: children as enthusiastic as ever, producing excellent drawing and clearly thinking about what they were seeing.

Banner making: Back at school Monday p.m. and Friday: designing banners and making these.  Again went well: a good group, thinking through their designs and listening and responding to advice about scale and layout.  In the end some of that gets lost and people try to fit tiny drawings onto huge bits of cloth and get frustrated when the masking tape resist process doesn't work well at that scale.  Overall, however, results were delightful and class felt very proud of themselves.

## Final stages: rehearsal and performance

On the last day before performance we rehearsed with the drama and puppet groups, with a final run-through on the actual day of performance.

## Extracts from workshop journal

Thursday 7th: Rehearsals with Drama and Puppet groups.  Entering today with some wariness after last week.  Take a deep breath and dive in... Morning: puppet group rehearsals: here we plunged in: just the morning to go from the story we all wrote to full action and we did it!  Group was wonderful, experimenting with their puppets, listening and trying out their animation and position, adding their individual stone people poems.

Afternoon: drama group had had a music session that morning with Pete (Teacher) and had put together a piece of music.  How did we feel about using this?  We said we'd try anything once or twice: more because the children had done it and had told their story again with their own sounds – but in many ways the timing was not right for the piece we had been working on.  However we persevered, shifting from their recorded piece to live music ('*technical team*' on percussion, me on bodhrán) at shadow puppets...

Single pieces of cloth for everyone work much better: fossilizing sandstone/sandstorm group look great: whirling and curling up in their sandstone forms.  Lava tends to be a bit slug-like: with more time might we have got more fluid movement here?  Mountains look positively macabre: black cowled figures accompanied by ghost-white glaciers.

Technical team of 5 provide lighting – stars and twinkling gems, music and arrival of comet.

Friday 8th: Morning: final run through all groups, heave sighs of relief and hope.

Afternoon: much running around...

The group performed to an audience made up of the rest of the school's pupils, perhaps thirty to forty parents, a school advisor and two staff from the Museum's education unit.

## Extracts from workshop journal
### Sequence

1. Banner entry: procession of fossil banners with biggest four unfolding as backdrop – look splendid on poles in the space of the hall.
2. Puppet show: I narrated while action unfolded and individual puppets added their *'this is me as a stone'* poems... group worked very well, taking cues and working together.
3. Story of the world – again worked very well. We nearly lost the glaciers at one point: they'd gone to sleep it seemed!... and of course, in front of an audience everyone rushed through their pieces a bit so we had some long pauses (problem with recorded music and no cues) but overall impact excellent and images powerful and lasting...

Audience very excited and lots of very positive feedback from visitors. At the end of the performance every child got a thank you *'certificate of exquisite artistry'*, based on one of J's drawings and signed by both L and myself.

## The Dance

*The world begins in darkness and the slow, slow movement of stone. Mountains growing, a craggy black silhouette, while yellow, red and orange lava flows, pouring through the darkness of rock. Stars twinkle on the edge of the world.*

*Time moves slowly.*

*Water flows across the face of the world, a rippling river of blue, and sandstorms whirl across the land, settling in dunes, swallowing shapes, fossilizing. Slow as slugs, glaciers slide up and drape themselves over the dark mountaintops. In the darkness at the foot of the mountains, coloured gems sparkle.*

*A flash of light and shadow puppets appear on a screen. Like an awkward television, images of animals and plants come and go, lingering for only a few moments, flickering memories in the lives of our stones.*

*A comet plunges out of the sky and the world breaks into turmoil. The shadow puppets have gone. Waters thrash and crash. Glaciers melt away. Mountains collapse. Lava pours back out and writhes across the world.*

*Time moves slowly.*

*The mountains grow again. The glaciers return.*

*Shapes under the sandstone stir and humans appear. Waking into their world, they stretch and look around. Taking their cloths they fold them, shaping stone into blocks, building a wall and coming to rest behind it.*

*The drama ends with stillness.*

## Did it work?

This is a difficult question to answer within the timeframe of a short project. Certainly, people were far more inspired by stones than we could have hoped and they threw themselves into it all with great enthusiasm. The imagination and concentration of performers in that final performance was a good measure for us of how committed they were to the event.

In the longer term, how much difference we make is always hard to tell. It is difficult to measure how much knowledge has been absorbed – and impossible to guess where an inspiration in stones may re-emerge or where it might take that person.

From discussion with the teachers and children and our own feelings as artists, a few definite thoughts emerge.

## Timescales

These did prove as tricky as we had expected. Perhaps the feeling of time running back and way out of human experience was best captured through stories.

For example: holding a stone in our hands and spinning time as an image, falling back past Victorians, past Tudors and Vikings and Romans, past Egyptians and Stonehenge, past Ice Ages, past mammoths, and Tyrannosaurus rex. Back and back through time, rolling back down centuries and millennia and aeons, back past memory and words, back until all we can do is dream and close our eyes and think of the silence before insects buzzed, before fish jumped, the stillness before jellyfish and sea anemones and crabs. Was the world empty before animals, or was it then the Stone's own world, the world of mountains crumbling slowly into sand, where everything lived the long slow life of stone? Dream.

## Clarity of geological knowledge

Within the timescale of the project, we did not have much time to work formally with stones and when we left the Museum, we left a lot of the hands-on material behind us.

While we had books to turn to and children researched their stones on the Internet, we felt – especially with the puppet group – that having samples and relevant information on each desk as people made their puppets and started developing the characters would have helped to connect stone and puppet much more clearly. As it was, while the children knew who and what their puppets were, it might not have always been quite so clear to an audience! Similarly with the main drama group, we could have used more time following processes. Perhaps video would have been helpful – something so that we could watch movement, something to remind us of colour and form in lava and glaciers, and the slow erosion of mountain to sand.

'More time' is a familiar call with school projects. 'More time' here could also have given us the opportunity to work with small groups within the main company, so we could focus on movement with the lava group folding with the mountain ranges and so on.

## Conclusion

Was the project successful in achieving its aims?

We were left with questions and wonderings: did we manage to embrace that sense of time? Were people left with a greater knowledge of geology? Would more time have made a big difference?

It is easy to be caught by the things that *'might have been different'*.

Given, however, that this was a pilot project, our test run to see if these activities could work and if people could engage with the whole set of concepts, then, yes, it was successful. The various art forms worked well individually in workshop and together in the final performance. In addition, we could see what sorts of geological resources would be needed on another occasion.

Most importantly, we saw that people will respond to the rocks of their home planet. There proved to be an excitement for stones lying inside people, waiting to be woken, waiting to be given a chance to come out to play.

*Time moves slowly.*
*The smallest survive and walk from their caves;*
*When the sun shows her face again.*
*With rocks in their hands;*
*With dreams in their minds;*
*They build a great city of stone.*
*Empires are built and battles are fought,*
*Each nation then has its own voice.*
*But the voice of the maker is written on stone,*
*And is smashed on a mountain by man.*

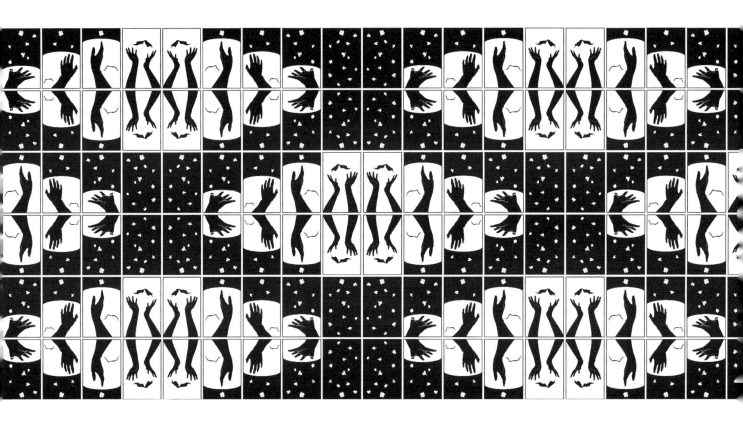

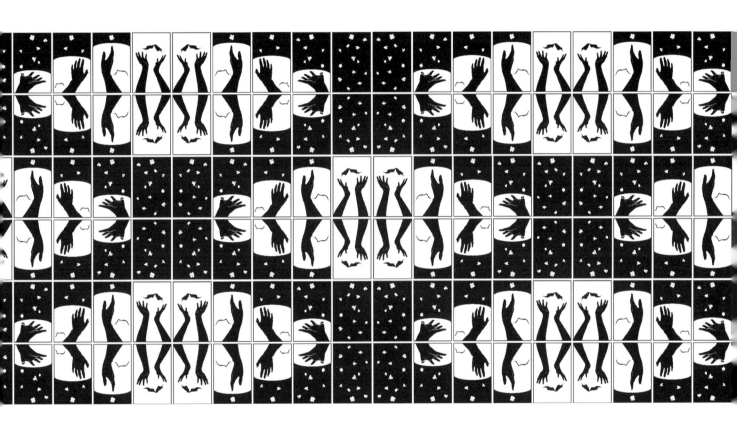

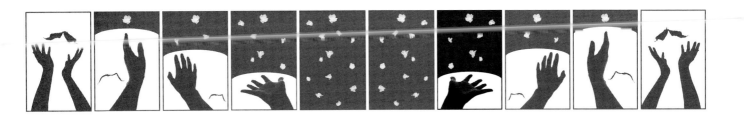

# Conclusion

Leslie Brown and Tom Mason

As parents and teachers we do our best to care for children's minds and lives. This, by necessity, means caring for the place where our children live – our home planet Earth. But it is only by studying Earth that we can truly get a sense of how deeply it has supported us.

At present, Earth is the only known haven of life in the universe. This is due to the life support systems on our planet, namely earth, air and water. We depend on these every moment of our existence. Each has a history and carries a story. What we are is a result of their common ancestry, an ancestry that may be hinted at by taking a walk through time. We hope that StarMatter will inspire you to take at least some footsteps on this walk.

We would like to leave you with some thoughts on our place within this story: where we have come from, how we interact with our planet, the issues and potential crises arising from this interaction, and, fundamentally, what we can do to celebrate this story and our place within it – considering the shadow cast by our economic and lifestyle choices.

## The universal story

Earth's story is but one strand in a far greater story – the story of our universe's creation and evolution, the story of Deep Time. This is not just an abstract concept. It can be seen every time we look up at the night sky or through a telescope. The further away from us that stars lie, the further back in time we see them, because their light takes time to reach us. As we look at the cosmos, we are in fact, looking back through time, as far back as fifteen to twelve billion years ago.

## Origin of life

In the history of life on Earth, the tenaciousness of life is apparent. Despite volcanic upheavals, cosmic bombardment, shifting continents and both shrinking and widening oceans, life has clung on. At many times in the past, the route taken by the evolution of life has been influenced by some disaster. At the end of the Permian, 250 million years ago, a catastrophe killed off 95% of marine organisms and 70% of terrestrial life, and an asteroid impact helped push the dinosaurs into extinction 65 million years ago. Both of these events helped drive the evolution of mammals along a specific route that has led to us. It is now generally accepted by mainstream science that life appeared very early in Earth history. Classic experiments in the early 1950's demonstrated that a mixture of gases, like those that would have been common in the atmosphere of the early Earth, when energized by electricity, produced a large variety of amino acids that are basic building blocks of life.

We also know of several inorganic mechanisms for concentrating the precursor chemicals of life. For example, when the ocean shallows are stirred up by strong winds to form the chemical flotsam that we call sea foam; or when hydrophilic minerals act as substrates where the inorganic chemicals that are necessary forerunners of life can be concentrated. These are ways in which chemicals could have been brought together on the surface of the young Earth. We now know that the precursor chemicals and some of the building blocks of life also exist in interstellar space, so ideas first formulated by Fred Hoyle about life being seeded on Earth from space may need more careful analysis.

Precursor chemicals include compounds that if we found them on Earth would be taken as indicators of the former existence of living organisms.

The discovery of deep-sea vent faunas living beyond the reach of sunlight along the volcanic seams of the Earth's oceans was the equivalent to finding aliens living on Earth. These chemo-synthesizers are very productive in terms of biomass, and clearly illustrate the blinkered viewpoint that can be caused by thinking Earth surface and sunlight for energy as the only solution for life. The further revelations about extremophile bacteria that survive in high temperature, hypersaline and other extreme environments has revived thoughts of finding life on Mars and on other bodies in the Solar System, namely the moons of Jupiter and Saturn. Only time will tell, but as long as we do not expect this alien life to be little green men, or anything else that we may hold a dialogue with, we may be pleasantly surprised to discover that living StarMatter has taken root in even odder places than our deep-sea vents.

We will likely discover that the most ubiquitous life in the Solar System may be biofilms. Any moist place in any hot part of the Earth is quickly colonized by slimy bacterial growth. Three and a half billion years ago bacterial-algal organic complexes built huge carbonate reefs (stromatolites) that were the largest biologically built structures on Earth. It is possible that bacteria are the ubiquitous life that we may discover beyond our planet.

## Geology and Gaia

The geology of planet Earth is steered by physical processes, lithospheric plate interactions, and the build-up of stresses in the crust that leads to enormous energy releases in earthquakes, the devastation of tidal waves, and the temporary catastrophic effects of floods, storms and tempests. The history of the planet is one of sudden convulsions and disasters, with a longer leavening of slow modification of landscapes born of cataclysms. We are now aware of the ever-present statistical danger of collision with extraterrestrial objects. Even quite small asteroids or comets contain enormous energy because of their hypervelocity and mass. An impact with Earth is capable of releasing enough energy to threaten our civilization: so we are now aware that apparently random events are capable of destroying us.

In this respect it is little wonder that we may consider our home planet to be a harsh place to live. Occasionally, like a dog scratching and shaking to rid itself of fleas, we may be forgiven for thinking of the Earth's convulsions as a way to rid itself of the pestilent organisms that are known as humans. Lovelock's hypothesis that the Earth is a self-regulating system suggests that Gaia's pulse may be the infrasound of the planet.

The planet is a finely tuned machine, responding to its ice ages and warm spells in a slow majestic way, until you look at the story that is told in the climatic records locked in ice preserved in the Polar Regions. These demonstrate that during the past the planet has reacted rather more swiftly than we thought possible to changes in oceanic circulation. The huge convection flows of the atmosphere and the conveyor belts of the deep oceans are the ameliorating factors that keep the climate fairly stable. But we now know that if they are switched off, like the North Atlantic Drift component of warm water from the tropics, then the coastlines of northwest Europe will freeze as hard as Labrador. Springtime in Paris may be somewhat delayed in this case. We know that this has happened before, for the history of humanity has been at the mercy of the continental ice sheets. At these times in the past, humans were scarce, and we were almost an endangered species.

The effect of pandemics on the human population is also a sobering lesson. The plagues of the 14th century slashed the European population, and our exposure to modern medical crises like the AIDS infection has provided a lesson that our greatest danger ironically may lie in the smallest inhabitants, and the longest-lived ones, on the planet. The true survivors are the bacteria and other tiny micro-organisms (Archaea).

## Life in space

It is now generally accepted by mainstream scientists that the depths of space may contain all of the building blocks necessary for life to start.

This is the coming of age of a theory first propounded by the astronomers Fred Hoyle and Chandra Wickramasingh who named it panspermia. They were ridiculed, as conventional wisdom at that time did not envisage this possibility. Since their proposal, the discovery of living organisms in the depths of Earth's oceans, thriving around hot springs, and deep underground in the interstitial spaces of rocks, and the ability of bacteria to survive the cold airless depths of interstellar space, has led to a dramatic shift in the paradigm for the limits of life.

The result of NASA's Viking Lander investigations of Martian soil for living organisms was seen as a set-back for those who believed that life ought to be common elsewhere in the universe. But these recent discoveries have clearly shown that we were not looking in the right place: the first few centimetres of the planet's surface are sterile, blasted by the solar wind and lethal UV radiation. It is now likely that the moons of the Solar System's gas giants may also be excellent targets for exobiologists.

## Life without oxygen

The realization that the Earth was not only rapidly seeded with life, but also that its water may well have been derived from cometary impacts during the early phases of the planet's history, has been one of the major changes in viewpoint of the scientific establishment. While still not generally accepted, the realization is slowly dawning that much of the change on Earth may be driven by external, that is to say, external to the Earth, forces. The first life forms were anaerobic as the atmosphere was lacking in oxygen. The stromatolites that thrived in the Earth's early oceans were colonies of blue-green algae and bacteria, sometimes called cyanobacterial colonies. An analogy today is that virtually anywhere on Earth where there is water and sunlight, a green slime will form. Biofilms are endemic on the modern planet's surface, and within its nooks and crannies. In the past these biofilms did not need oxygen, but generated it as a by-product of their simple metabolism. It took millions of years for the steady oxygen production of the stromatolite colonies to sweep all of the dissolved iron from the Earth's oceans. Once this was accomplished, the build up of oxygen, and eventually the formation of ozone, were necessary precursors for the evolution of multi-cellular life forms that were able to colonize the shallow oceans. The lure of the intertidal habitat and the food supplies that were promised by the abundant flush of early vegetation probably drove the evolution of animals that colonized the land. So the drive may have been food, and the ever-present push into pristine habitats, the eternal quest for the evolutionary advantage.

We also note that the first compounds to seed the Earth and prime it for life processes were carbon-based amino acids and other complex hydrocarbons. They arrived on the planet's surface in carbonaceous chondrites, a type of meteorite that is now relatively uncommon, but which represents samples of the early stuff that coalesced to make the planets circling the sun. This is the stuff of the life cycles of stars. It is also noteworthy that the oxidative removal of soluble iron from the Earth's oceans also represents the mopping up of starstuff: for it is iron that is the critical element in the life cycle of stars. Its accumulation in a star's nuclear core, allied to the mass of the star, determines whether they become hot white dwarfs or cool red giants. The heavier rarer elements that we prize most, like gold and platinum, and the even weightier radioactive transuranics, which may yet spell out our fate, are the products of supernovae. So truly there is no escape from the evidence of our stellar origin.

## The Drake Equation

The statistics and probabilities of the Drake equation are most compelling. The Drake Equation is a mathematical formula that calculates how many communicating civilizations may exist in the Universe besides ours.
The equation is written technically as follows:

$$N = R \times f_p \times n_e \times f_l \times f_i \times f_c \times L$$

$N$   is the number of communicative civilizations

$R$   is the rate of formation of suitable stars

$f_p$   is the fraction of these stars with planets

$n_e$   is the number of 'Earths' per planetary system

$f_l$   is the fraction of those planets where life develops

$f_i$   is the fraction of sites where intelligent life develops

$f_c$   is the fraction of planets where technology develops

$L$   is the lifetime of communicating civilizations

When we consider that our galaxy contains around 100 billion stars, and that there are billions of galaxies in the known universe, the statistical probability of intelligent life being a unique phenomenon of Earth seems counterintuitive and plainly wrong. If we remove the last three of the functions of this equation, in other words, simply considering the evolution of life, but not necessarily intelligence, technology or civilization, the statistics become compelling. Life may be liberally sprinkled throughout the cosmos: but it is unlikely to be worried about us, or to have the ability to think.

Given the common distribution of the elements and chemicals that are the building blocks of life in deep space and in the star nurseries of the gassy dusty nebulae, it therefore appears to be highly unlikely that we are alone in the universe. It is evident that life on Earth has flourished and colonized almost every available niche: why should this not be so elsewhere?  On our 24-hour clock scheme it is also obvious that the development takes place at a relatively rapid rate, and that it is punctuated by crises, sometimes extra terrestrially derived.

It has been stated in the past that unicellular life may have evolved many times on the early Earth, and that it only took one longer-term success to make sure that the bridgehead was not capable of being dislodged.  But for all of this to have happened, the Earth had to have water.  Life as we understand it, no matter where on Earth it is found, is a phenomenon of water.  That is what makes our planet unique within the Solar System: our lifeboat in space is blue, a water planet, and without it we would be a dry dusty desert like Mars, or a runaway high temperature greenhouse planet like Venus.  Consider it, and marvel.

Our planet is only one of billions of planets, suns and stars within the truly vast setting of the universe, an almost inconceivably long story. Yet this setting affects us on a daily basis.  The sun provides the entire energy needed by the Earth, be it through direct sunlight or energy stored in fossil fuels, which captured the sunlight of millions of years ago.  Water and wind power – two key elements of our life support systems – also derive all their energy from the sun, which stirs the atmosphere's winds, and raises the clouds of vapour that fall as rain.

A marvellous film, Solarmax, which portrays the *'song of the sun'*, can be seen at the IMAX cinema in the Science Museum, London.  Here we can see how the Sun continually throws out enormously energetic flares.  Occasionally these are particularly long and interfere with the power and electronic systems on which much of our economy and activity depends.  This happens at particular times of the year.

Another Deep Time relationship exists between the Earth and the Moon, and also affects life and living things on our planet.  We are still not precisely sure how the Moon formed – by its own separate accretion at the time of Earth's accretion, followed by its capture by the Earth, or by a meteorite or asteroid striking the Earth soon after the latter's core had formed and breaking off a large piece of the mantle. But we do know that the Moon supplies the driving gravitational influence on the oceans' tides.  If there were no tides in the oceans of Earth, life may not have followed the evolutionary path that has led to us.

## The Earth's story

We are accustomed to history lessons – the story of emerging man, the formation of nations, civilizations, and people of diverging race.  Mankind's curiosity and ingenuity was brought to bear over thousands of years to unravel the story of the universe's history. How that story has changed and grown during that time!

With our effective deciphering of a kind of an *alphabet of creation*, we may now attempt histories of our own planet and its life support systems – water, soil, atmosphere, biosphere, and so on. Some of these histories have been simplified for a less scientific audience and are available as books and videos from the BBC.

There is a certain irony in the fact that aspects of our extractional economy have equipped us to identify and appreciate our sense of position within the Sacred Balance described by David Suzuki. For example, to foster children's enthusiasm and sense of creativity about the Earth, we can draw on aspects of Deep Time and Deep Life. Using the spectacular Hubble Space Telescope images to journey backwards in time, we are able to unravel a fraction more of the history of the Solar System and the Earth.

It is important to mention that a popular view of science as being somehow cast in stone is totally erroneous. All science, the hypotheses, deductions and conclusions are continuously challenged and modified as new information comes to light. Science is characterized by its continuous flux of upgrade and change. Over the course of time, many stories of our universe's formation – both scientific and theological – have slipped into myth and legend. This is not necessarily a downgrading: myth is a vital vehicle for certain truths that cannot be expressed at the time in any other way. Moreover, while elements of these stories may be adapted or left behind in the pursuit of truth, they sometimes provide the foundations upon which later superstructures are built. In other words, while our contemporary scientific findings may well become myths of the future, we should not encourage reverence only for the latest insights.

## The stories of our life support systems

The relationship between our biosphere and other aspects of our planet has evolved over billions of years. This indicates a number of key concepts – the common ancestry shared by minerals, organisms and celestial bodies; the high degree of interconnectedness (and interdependence) between life forms and natural life support systems on our planet; and the need for organisms to adapt in order to survive.

Like our planet, we humans are made of water, air and numerous elements. The very elements within our body – like those in our planet – were formed in outer space and in several successive generations of stars by the processes of nucleosynthesis long before planetary accretion took place. Everything within and upon planet Earth, including ourselves, is made of StarMatter.

It is now suggested that life on Earth, including us, evolved from bacteria, a life form many of us now prefer to scrub off our hands or sweep away under a carpet. In the cells of our bodies, our powerhouse mitochondria originated as separate organisms that later became secondary components of our cellular structure.

**Air** – our atmosphere – is one of our three life support systems. Without the oxygen it provides, we would die. While countless aerobic creatures and we ourselves depend on this oxygenated atmosphere, others, including our earliest bacterial ancestors, prefer anaerobic atmospheres: to them, oxygen is a poisonous gas. In the planet's early days, oxygen made up less than 1% of our atmosphere's constitution.

It is a twist of fate that our anaerobic ancestors created the atmosphere in which we live – but which poisons them. To survive, they needed either to adapt or die. Unless they found another habitat they would have perished, thereby transforming them into some other form of StarMatter, be it animate or inanimate.

The atmosphere will continue to evolve over time, affected to some extent by our own activity. For example, at the moment we are increasing $CO_2$ levels. The same rules, which governed what happened to anaerobic bacteria, will apply to aerobic organisms that over time find themselves in an anaerobic environment – as we may do if the constitution of our atmosphere changes. Again, the choice is to adapt, find another habitat, or die and be transformed into elemental StarMatter.

**Soil** is another of our life support systems, created by the interaction of rock with sun and rain. Later, the activity of bacteria and lichens breaks it down further; later still larger creatures such as worms and rodents further re-cycle and work it. Over time, these processes have gradually produced soil with a high percentage of humus, or organic matter.

We can see how our bacterial ancestors were as involved in the formation of the soil system, as much as they were involved in the formation of our atmosphere. Yet what is our response? Every year, the natural fertility of precious topsoil is being depleted by modern farming practices and excessive irrigation, among other factors.

**Water** is the third of our life support systems. We are not certain of its origin on Earth – perhaps it was conveyed to Earth from extraterrestrial sources via multiple impacts of icy comets, perhaps it was derived from the dewatering of minerals within the Earth appearing as steam from active volcanoes. The subtle balance between water and landmass on our planet has changed throughout time, having a profound bearing on how life forms developed and evolved into species. The salination and desalination of water has also impacted on the pattern of life. The most adaptable creatures survive these changes while the others don't.

## The human eco-footprint: opening out our worldview

Many believe we have temporarily conquered part of the Earth's crust with our concrete jungles. Some believe we can master the air and will soon exploit space travel. We fuel these activities with nature's precious reservoir of fossil fuels. Too often, *'modern man'* has viewed himself as separate to nature, thus disregarding the universe's interconnectedness.

However, a rapidly increasing number of people, and not only the young, have been concerned for at least two decades that changes are necessary in the way our ever increasing populations live their lives. Now, more than ever, it is vital to encourage the momentum and will for change. To-date, world education has been predominantly, and perhaps inevitably, anthropocentric, having little concern for the role that the *'other than human'* influences play by the very fact that we are here, alive and in a position of consciousness. Some would say that at times even our anthropocentric emphasis falls short, in that it hasn't sufficiently honoured cultures other than one's own. We conduct our lives often neglectful of nature's power, reminded only in a fearful way by the nightly news bulletins which detail the loss of life due to earthquakes, tidal waves and floods.

However, is there a more positive way to interact and understand the natural sphere, the *'other than human'*? Can we expand our perception so that we can find a way to appreciate fully the scale, intensity of temperature and transformative processes fundamental within the universe with a view to changing both our worldview and the way we live our lives?

## The interconnectedness of nature

The last century witnessed the identification of, amongst other systems, the biosphere, the atmosphere and the stratosphere. We now recognize these as interdependent entities, each of which affects and depends on the others. StarMatter has reflected this perspective in exploring not just the geological structure of our planet, but also the story of its origins in relation to the biosphere and the greater universal drama of which it is a part.

The need for recycling is now recognized on an international level. Our modern waste is significantly less biodegradable and less recyclable than that of previous generations. Our modern lifestyles and technology mean that our commodities have to travel from further a field to us, and are often packaged in compound ways, with wire and plastic. This renders it harder to dispose of each material separately.

Fewer households in the developed world now feed scraps to farm animals, with the result that ever more organic treasures intermingle with toxins that are dumped in landfills. The sites chosen for the landfills are often on agricultural land, which thus becomes unusable for many a year – time way beyond our children's children's lifetime. Little regard was given to this when setting these landfills until we began to comprehend the interconnected underground water networks on which they rest.

Recently we began to recognize the role of the aquifers that carry leached toxic waste. Water, being an excellent solvent, gathers toxins and transports them away. As these fingers of water disperse from the landfill in a complex and distant pattern, they affect the life support systems way beyond the local area.

So, not only is the landfill polluting local soil, it could be bad news to neighbouring homes and farms. It is important at this stage to acknowledge the steps that are being taken to counter water pollution. For example, there is a Welsh firm, which has developed a process that allows urban sewage water in the developing world to be used for irrigation. Similar water recycling is also taking place in China. European Union compliant groundwater protection schemes have been introduced in Ireland. There is an extensive range of hydrogeological and thematic maps on aquifer vulnerability, pollution, acid rain susceptibility and geothermal potential, some of which can be viewed on-line.

As our holistic perceptions re-awaken, we also become aware of the various implications of these contaminants in air, soil and water. No wonder that we are somewhat overwhelmed at our vulnerability, as our consumer society – and our methods of recycling the vast amount we consume – come full circle and end up by affecting someone else, if not ourselves.

The forces of nature have more powerful methods of transportation than hitherto understood. Nothing can be taken away that does not come back in some form, at some point in time. Our own life support systems are becoming tampered with as sand and dust travel from one continent to the other with airborne diseases. Incinerators also pose problems of toxicity and contamination.

## An extractional economy

We have examined the cycles of life that have taken place on our planet since its formation. We have looked at how species formed, adapted, survived and died out; how the very texture of Earth has evolved and changed since its early days. This brings us on to our own cycle and how, through it, we are interacting with the planet we live on and with. We leave our *'eco-footprint'*, the mark we leave on the surface and interior of Earth as we evolve and grow.

Many children are no longer raised in the countryside. Being effectively decoupled from much of the nature that would have been their teacher in past generations, they remain ignorant of farming practices, and of the way modern farming methods greatly reduce the quality and quantity of precious topsoil. The materialism of our lives results in even more disposable waste, much of which is packaging. Ours is what Thomas Berry would call *"an extractional economy"*.

There is debate as to when we as a species developed this particular eco-footprint. It is thought that some of our ancestors – possibly before and at the time of the hunter-gatherers – lived *'lightly'* with the Earth, causing much less disruption of the Sacred Balance concept promoted by Suzuki. However, there has been some debate on the extent to which early hominids had a devastating effect on the large plains animals. It is probably therefore fair to say that particularly in the last two hundred years, with the human population explosion and the Industrial Revolution, we began taking far more from the Earth than we gave back.

Not least is the issue of our population: that two billion people are now without most of the basic necessities of life – and this doesn't refer to a pebbledash semi, shiny car and 2.4 children. The current human population exceeds 6 billion, and is growing at a rate of about 1.7% per annum, if this growth continues, the total in 100 years will be a staggering 30 billion. Clearly something must give, and the greatest impact is likely to be damage to the biosphere. When China annually adds the population of Holland to its already huge total, we must expect some strain on the planet's resource base. We must recognize there is urgency to seriously tackle these issues: energy and water are two of the key problem areas, as is, of course, food production. Our homes, farming practices, population and methods of travel all bear witness to our eco-footprint, the degree to which we disrupt, or kill, or force to adapt the *'world of others'* as we focus on building our human-centred world. To quote James Lovelock, writing in a letter; *"We live with, not on, the planet."* One effect of our extractional economy is that it may accelerate fundamental changes in the life support system of our planet. These changes take time to ascertain and are not always reversible. For example, contamination and overuse of our groundwater is a problem of which future generations will become increasingly aware.

## Minimal impact

Nature is cyclical: planets accrete and in time break up, or become radically transformed: species come and go. It therefore makes sense to realize that our sojourn on the planet is ephemeral. Too often our own illusions of permanence blind us to this realization. But once we do wake up we must ask the obvious question: how can we live in order to make the best of our limited stay? There are conflicting suggestions as to exactly how simply we should live in order to make minimal impact of the planet. A lot depends on how many of us inhabit Earth. Also, how much energy we should be using other than solar, wind and water energy, so as to put a stop on our draining of nonrenewable fuel resources.

According to Edward O. Wilson writing in '*The Future of Life*':

> "*The choice is clear: the juggernaut [of technology-based capitalism] will very soon either chew up what remains of the living world, or it will be redirected to save it.*" (p.156.)

Wilson points out the importance of maintaining a high level of biodiversity – a spread of life forms across habitats. In previous chapters, we saw how biodiversity naturally comes and goes, as the planet passes through its own life cycles. However, at this time we are actively, if unconsciously, reducing biodiversity – through factors like monoculture modern farming methods, immigration patterns and over-use of natural, non-renewable resources such as the rainforests.

## Addressing the imbalance

So, given the generally destructive nature of our impact on our life support systems – and given our brief position in the story not only of these systems but also of the planet and universe – what can we do?

The question is really twofold: how do we address the damage we have done while at the same time celebrating aspects of our existence?

## Celebrating the dance of the universe

Since the beginning of recorded history, the agenda and mysterious dance of the universe has attracted many interpretations. People throughout history have debated, philosophized and wondered about the marvel of the life we are blessed with on this privileged planet. Many have wondered at the purpose behind it all, and generations of human beings have woven aspects of Deep Time into their collective and personal stories.

Many plays, songs, games and other creative adventures could be devised from the phenomena we have described in preceding chapters, resulting in new representations of children's cosmological education. We have described one such approach in our case study.

So that children better understand their place within the Deep Time frame, parents and/or teachers could emphasize both the didactic and the celebratory aspects of this kind of learning. In other words, children would be taught techniques that could lead to a '*lighter*' way of living on the planet, while at the same time being encouraged to celebrate the fleeting nature of their existence as individuals and a species.

## Personification

The power of personification has proved throughout time to be of great value. Myths and legends abound with figures of Earth goddesses, water gods and fiery rulers of underground kingdoms. Astronomy outreach in particular has used this technique most effectively. It is possible for our children to personify attributes of Deep Time in a similar way through role-play.

Personification and cosmological character can take different forms: giant puppets – as we saw in the case study – cartoon animation or people impersonating concepts such as gravity. Pie charts could provide a quick reference to percentages of elements, water, soil, oxygen and so on.

The real surprise for both children and educators is probably the degree of interconnectedness, not just with each other genetically, but with other species, elements, particles and forces within nature in the Deep Time Universe. Everything within our planet has StarMatter as common ancestry. Each element has a story. Some are set in deeper time than others, hydrogen and helium being the two oldest to become established as we now know them. Particles such as photons, electrons, quarks and neutrinos could also be dramatized; as their dynamic nature and the constantly shifting relationships they enjoy offer tremendous potential for movement and drama.

If we personify elements, then gravity and energy could equally be included in the drama. The universe is held together by gravity. Energy varies in its manifestation, from the unimaginable intensity of the Big Bang to the softly drifting cloud.

Or we could take the example of water, a very important character in the story of Earth. Pie charts inform us of the percentage of ground water and surface water – which we depend on for survival – to ice and salty seas. Each form of water could be personified. Further characters could include an aquifer, water-depleted land (possibly due to overpopulation and poor water management) and various individual water molecules – some of which are toxic from landfills, some acid rain, some tainted by industrial dyes, others dew drops, as used by desert people.

Different phase characteristics of water could also be illustrated by characters; for example solution, or sublimation. In the latter case, several people could play cloud, mist, sleet, snow and ground frost. Equally, we could personify the timescale in which stocks of water are replaced or replenished. For example, one person could play time, another a certain length of Deep Time in which water is overused, while a third character or group plays a desert, which scatters itself about the stage, while in the distance the heavy plodding of the appropriate Deep Time overtaking the desert is heard.

## Literature and the Earth sciences

Another area of creative activity, which could be explored in the context of the Earth Sciences, is literature. The Earth and its land-, sea- and air-scapes (lithosphere, hydrosphere and atmosphere) have inspired poets, novelists, playwrights and scientific writers since the beginning of the written word. It seems natural for literature to go a few steps further into actively celebrating the story of our Earth.

In the classroom, creative writing could include science topics such as cosmology and Earth sciences. Thus science could become an imaginative exploration linked closely with expression in print. Scripts and poems, essays and bullet point research items could be more actively addressed to include these areas.

As Wittgenstein and other philosophers have indicated, thought and language are almost inextricably linked. A new thought can create a new word; changing the language we use can affect the way we think. This is borne out in disciplines such as Neuro-Linguistic Programming, where even deep-seated attitudes and habits can be changed slowly through an awareness and modification of the language we use.

Careful note could therefore be made of the basic vocabulary at the heart of the Earth story and its cosmology, which derives mostly from the scientific facts of the last one hundred and fifty years. Examples of relevant vocabulary that spring to mind include acid rain, climate change, sustainability and biodiversity. From the economic perspective, authors such as Amory Lovins, co-author of Factor Four suggest that we need to rethink – and reword – the way we measure and quantify economic activity. They posit that design and technology should be based on *resource efficiency* and that judging an economy on the rate of its growth and expansion is both outdated and ecologically destructive. Instead they propose a sort of green GDP. This would take into account long and medium term costs of economic activity on the environment and a broader and more equitable notion of *welfare*.

Other examples of this new vocabulary include *living lightly*, *sustainable growth*, *appropriate technology*", *people-centred economics* and *one-world versus the wealth-of-nations economic models*.

Because of this – and because of our accelerating population – different variables, such as safe air, water and soil, will become priorities in the future, as will wholesome food. From time immemorial, wars have been fought over the use of the Earth's resources; as our population rises and puts pressure on these resources, new wars will probably be fought over some of our life support systems.

## Bioregional studies

As a practical study of ways to live more *'lightly'*, bioregional studies could be examined and encouraged amongst communities. These would facilitate their awareness of their own surroundings, its immediate changing history, its ecology and its immediate future, bearing in mind our relative eco-footprints on this region.

It is important that this kind of study discusses not just human footprints, but also nature's transformative qualities, which is a different kind of footprint. Thus we will be making a distinction between the natural activities of our planet and factors that are unusual and involve our contribution. It would be interesting to introduce Schumacher's concepts discussed in *'Small is Beautiful'*. There are several institutions carrying out aspects of his work.

*'Creating sustainable cities'* is an issue that may become urgent: as fuel prices soar, we will no longer be able to afford cheap food imports. We may already be experiencing this price escalation. Some economies are already researching and implementing long-term cleaner fuel strategies as for example, China. Many European countries have less far-sighted forward strategies. There is also the potential of *'leapfrog'* strategies, whereby developing countries may be able to bypass the pollution issues of the developed world by immediately using cleaner, cheaper fuel.

Through these kinds of studies, children could develop a practical understanding of the value of the local community and maintaining basic life skills within it – as well as being recipients of commodities and technologies that come from afar. It would surely be exciting for the new generations to become familiar with living machines, farms created within cities in town buildings and methods for preserving and creating topsoil for those who do not own farmland. This would allow children to maintain a familiarity with the source of their food that comes directly from nature.

## A final word

In StarMatter, we seek to offer a glimpse of our ancestry as it is described in science. By simplifying certain concepts through artistic outreach and creativity, we hope to encourage a sense of gravity, enthusiasm and wonder for children of the future. We also hope that this project will make the subject matter accessible to educators and parents; and that it will encourage teachers and parents to use local experts as well as exploring the many *'science-made-simple'* books available in the educational market – while bearing in mind that a non-holistic slant can be even more common in some popular science books and encyclopaedias.

Many topics such as loss of biodiversity, pollution and shortage of clean drinking water can become overwhelming to children. But by acting out, writing about and researching these areas, they can be empowered with an alternative vision – and, hopefully, practice – for the future.

The Deep Life, Deep Time emphasis we touch on is not commonly in school curricula – although we believe it is highly relevant to children of the

21st century, affording them a wider, more universal perspective and understanding of history. We believe this jump can be facilitated even for young children, once their teachers have carried out appropriate research.

## Mythical tools

We are conscious that the science tools we are using in this outreach may be deemed mythical within a short time; certainly, they will need to be adapted and developed. We may be humbled to learn that the Egyptian pyramids, and the Newgrange tomb in Ireland, have revealed that their architects were keen astronomers, while certain aspects of modern computer science refer back to ancient mathematical formulae carved in stone.

Our new technologies offer us fascination and precision. Over centuries, academic disciplines have created the building blocks for our current perception. However, other peoples have for centuries worked around many related concepts with many different theologies and philosophies. In South Africa an extensive human history is memorised and recounted through the oral tradition, rather than in written form.

This resembles the Song lines of the Aborigines. The iconography of many peoples reveals much more complex and sophisticated structures than we, who rely on the written word for communication, may realize. Imagine representing the different forms of memory through role-play, including a store of memorized stories; the developed world would probably figure as a person carrying a computer in place of the aboriginals' mental stories.

## Gazing at the stars

The intent of StarMatter is to facilitate outreach for children organized by adults. Children's minds are often more open and receptive to absorb a wide range of information. Adults sometimes carry the burden of conditioning and thus may be less receptive. However, both children and adults suffer the consequences of our unregulated experimentation on our life support systems, soil, air and water.

We have to ensure that today's children are able to stand on the grass and gaze and understand something of the stars, not relying entirely on computers. We hope the above efforts will enable both teachers and children to celebrate greater Earth literacy and better understand the characteristics and extraordinary changes these creatures, elements and forces reveal during their existence.

## Holistic approach

StarMatter's strong emphasis is on a holistic approach, something that is not always encouraged in the rush and complexity of specialization. Either a reductionist or an overly specialist approach can mean that experts, even within the same discipline, are unable to communicate with each other on their said topic; in this way the bigger vision is lost.

By its nature, StarMatter's interdisciplinary approach bridges some of these gaps with the inclusion of Deep Time, Deep Life. We hope to promote a broader vision within the educational blueprint; to encourage development and a sense of self, enthusiasm and open-mindedness through each individual's creativity. For example, by giving art students a brief related to Earth Science subjects, they could be learning about the science while perfecting their artistic skills. The same could be done in literature courses by choice of book and assignment. Some music composers, for example Paul Winter, have already addressed the extinction of species in their compositions and public performances.

Many theatre groups and body and voice workshops have already begun exploring these areas. We offer an introduction to the multiplicity of this approach and a confirmation that it can be both beneficial and educational. It is thus no longer a question of can it be done, rather who will do it, and how and where?

Maybe the elements of our civilization, which have brought us to this place in our history, can offer us a way forward. Now that human culture is seen increasingly as a global one, it may be possible for us all – scientists and artists, parents and teachers, activists and politicians – to meet afresh on the *'common ground'* of the best of human aspirations. Perhaps we can now work toward a shared vision of those basic things that all mankind agrees upon. This is one path, which seems to extend from the shared *'science'* vision that the world now has – and which has only recently come into being.

All involved in this project have had inspiring teachers. Their presence has cultivated a sense of wonder and curiosity. We hope that StarMatter is a reflection of this.

### *It takes a Universe*

*The child awakens to a universe.*

*The mind of the child to a world of meaning.*

*Imagination to a world of beauty.*

*Emotions to a world of intimacy.*

*It takes a universe to make a child*

*Both in outer form and inner spirit.*

*It takes a universe to educate a child.*

*A universe to fulfil a child.*

© Thomas Berry

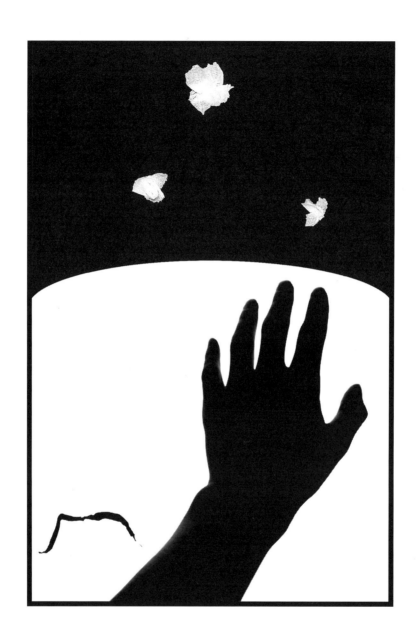

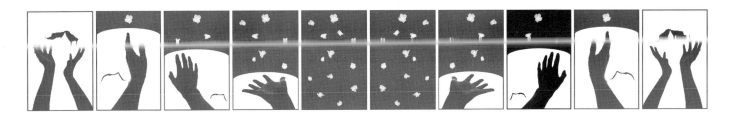

# Flashes of Inspiration

Gordon MacLellan

A Life of Stone offered a detailed exploration of one project but we suggest that a similar degree of creative examination can be brought to bear on many of the subjects discussed in StarMatter.

This chapter presents some ideas, large and small, for embarking on Deep Time, Deep Life journeys with groups. Work from three different environmental arts and interpretation workers is brought together to outline three bigger projects that you might want to use as they are, or perhaps these ideas will simply spark off your own and you will explore somewhere else? At the end there is a small blizzard of other ideas: schemes these artists and other StarMatter workers have brewed that just might launch you on another adventure. Here we will consider:

❖ Evolution, looking at the growth and change of life on our planet using shadow puppets drawing on work by the same Creeping Toad who coordinated 'A Life of Stone'.

❖ A sense of time, using poetry and narratives from poet and writer Susan Cross.

❖ Bacteria, thrilling to microbes from the 'Theatre in Schools' work of Ruth Brocklehurst.

These examples will be considered as if being worked with school groups and presented in forms that, while not closely conforming to the British National Curriculum, are not so very remote from it that teachers would not see any value in the work. Other countries and other situations will have other priorities so what follows are simply suggestions. Use these to lay the keels of the boats of your own imagination.

## Evolution: a life in headlines!

Our planet is rich in life, rolling in a bewildering wonder of diversity both past and present. It is easy to get caught by the large and obviously spectacular, both when looking at modern biodiversity and at the fossil record. You could discuss the idea of 'charismatic megafauna' with your group.  Now, these may be whales and elephants, lions and tigers.  From the past dinosaurs, mammoths and sabre-toothed cats are obvious examples.  But the real richness of life may lie in the small things, and while less obvious and hard to see, the fossil remains of the little creatures are truly wondrous.  If you can draw your group into a consideration of these you might end up with a much more exciting shadow puppet performance than one dominated by large carnivorous reptiles punctuated by occasional Neanderthals and woolly mammoths.

This project was planned as a one-day workshop for 12-16 year olds.

Exploring evolution through key moments and changes, leading to a shadow puppet performance with different stages captured in the shadow action and projected newspaper headlines of the time.  This has made for lively and very entertaining events, where the levity of the final performance belies the depth of work and understanding behind it.

1. Situation: a day workshop for ~30 students, including that final performance.  The time could be split over several sessions on different days allowing the performance more rehearsal time.

2. Setting and sources: this workshop works well in a museum context with access to interesting evolutionary displays, and handling collections where students can work in small groups to do their own detective work.  In schools or other settings, you will need to carefully assemble information packs for the participants.

3. Activities: the introductory activity is evolution in bits. The challenge is to assemble an evolutionary timeline from a set of *'headlines'*. Several sets of these are needed so that the company can break into smaller groups with room for everyone to participate and discuss. Recognize that your *'headlines'* here may well set the tone for what comes later, so think carefully and aim for perhaps 20 headlines.  You might want to supply a printed stratigraphic column for support and suggestions.

Sample headlines are, in no particular order:
*"Primeval soup thickens: life imminent!"*;
*"A Nucleus gives my life shape,"* says microbe;
*"Feet will never catch on,"* says fish;
*"Throw off your shells!"* (first octopus);
*"I am someone else's bad dream"* (Hallucigenia from the Burgess Shale);
*"It'll miss!"* (dinosaur on meteorite);
*"We survived"*, exclaims shrew;
*"We will fight them for the beaches"* (amphibian);
*"Flowers are decadent"* (coniferous plants).

And so it begins.

## Evolution detectives

Working with museum collections or other materials, students assemble their own timelines. It might help to assign groups to particular time periods or habitats and set them to look for significant *'headline'* events. Then try jigsawing these different findings together. See if the company can find themes running through their different findings: the rise and fall of reptiles, the changing patterns of life in the sea. It can become bewilderingly diverse so, to focus rambling ideas a bit, you might turn to what was happening in your own area over time, tying changing life forms with changes in your own geology.

## First shadows

Experiment with quick cardboard cut-outs. Use strong card and add a single joint (try paper fasteners or thread) and move a head or limb or flex an early spine. Cut patterns within the main shape and colour with acetate, gel or tissue. Introduce growth with tubes and sticks to push or strings to pull so plants may grow or tube worms and corals fan out. The simplest shadow screen is made by suspending a sheet and pulling it tight at the corners and sides. A small halogen-bulb desk lamp makes a good light source. You might make a frame and stretch a cotton screen across this, but a large screen allows for easy changing from one scene to another, especially as this will almost certainly mean a change of puppeteers as well.

## Main assignment

Now let groups go: make sure each group has a time period with a brief to decide for themselves the most significant events within that headline (see below). Start making shadow puppets that show changes (lobe-finned fish sprout legs, an amoeba squeezes itself into a cell wall).

   This sounds simple but it calls for precise work and clear thinking. Discoveries need to be distilled down to specific moments and the impact of these captured in a phrase or two.

## Headlines

These might be written on card and held up in *'silent movie'* style or prepared on acetate sheets and projected on the puppet screen or thrown by an overhead projector onto another screen. The latter allows for other experimentation with colours and the moving patterns of ink and crystal dissolution as *'special effects'*.

## Experiment

With colour and texture within the puppet (feathers, leaves, fur and hair might all help), focus (distance of puppet from screen) and background music.

## Simplicity

Always encourage your groups to keep their section simple.  It is easy to crowd the shadow puppet stage with so much action that the audience misses the crucial moment.

## Continuity

The final performance might be delivered as a set of *'bullet-points'*, or the group might consider having a narrator linking stages, making more of a *'story'* of it, or follow the course of time through one small creature that crawls across every scene, observing, surviving and never changing.  This is also an opportunity to explore other images of *'linear'* time.  Familiar representations include the history of the Earth on a 24-hour clock, or you might try a calendar format or a countdown (what happens when the clock reaches 00:00?).  Be wary of using the arrival of humanity as a final moment or even as a highpoint in evolution.  We are almost certainly only one moment in that ongoing flow of life.  We are not the endpoint and as for a highpoint... well, dinosaurs were bigger, Burgess Shale and Precambrian life more bizarre, and so many things more beautiful and just about everything else more sensible than we have been yet!

## Final performance

Stop and think and make an occasion of the event.  Devise a title, find some useful music to set the scene, or to run behind everything else that happens.  Slow the action down, use the music for rhythm in your shadow movement.  Dress your puppeteers (uniform black is useful).  Recruit an audience.  Fellow students are always useful and in a museum setting, try putting up a poster at lunchtime and simply go for it at the end of the day.  Set out chairs.  Welcome the audience.  Introduce the performance and at the end invite the performers to come out and take a bow.  Recognize and celebrate achievement.

## Stone poems

Poet Susan Cross suggests ways of looking beyond rocks and into changing landscapes and a sense of geological time.

Start with the familiar and the immediate.  She writes:

> *"I write with stones on my desk.*
>
> *There are mysterious minerals doing magical things in and behind the screen I am writing on.  These words are appearing from the rock.*

*I come from a farming family and there is soil in my blood.*

*Rocks lie, like the bones of my body at the core of everything I see and know."*

So start with the stones around us. Ask your group to think about their connection to stone, of all the places where they use rocks and minerals. This needs to range from the obvious (houses, perhaps) to the unexpected (talcum powder?).

The activities that follow work with a group sitting in a room fingering through a tray of rocks or with a group exploring a hillside and encountering boulders.

## Time to listen to a rock

❖ Susan reminds us that to write powerfully we need to write from our hearts. We need to listen heart to heart to the rock in our hands. The first and most obvious thing about listening to rocks is timescale. There is such a contrast between their lifetimes and ours, maybe they take only one breath during all the time you or I might be born, grow old and die. Rock is not likely to babble at us. Think of the one sentence your rock might say during your lifetime. You may have to almost drift off to sleep beside your rock to get an answer. Sometimes, very talkative rocks like shale may give you a whole Haiku. Others like a solid granite or ponderous basalt may just mutter the odd syllable or two.

❖ Rock verbs (and verbs rock!). It is the verbs, the words that describe action and being, that make writing vivid. Not the adjectives that can clog it up but the verbs. So try writing about your rock in verbs only. At first you may find yourself using verbs of inaction like lying, sitting or standing. Be patient. Reach back into stone's past. Go back through time and find how this rock has changed. There, you may find words like swell, melt, flow, rise, surf on waves of strata, dissolve, fall, split, glitter, crush, smother. The life story of a rock is full of drama and in drama we find interesting writing.

❖ Research. This would be a good time to spend some time exploring and find out how and where your rock formed, what it has been through to reach the form you now find it in.

❖ Rocks are lively: as you start writing your rock's life story, avoid passive verbs like *'it was carried by glaciers'* and think of the events in your rock's life as adventures. Perhaps your rock *'rode on glaciers'* or *'bathed, melting in the magma'*. Try also staying in the present, describing things as if they were happening now. Once you have the verbs you can start building the whole story. But be strict and ration the number of other words you can use. Give yourself a word diet. Cut out adverbs completely. Where you find a verb needs a description, maybe you could

find a more appropriate verb.  Maybe your verbs will need no other words at all, but can stand alone in a terse but action packed sequence as if the words themselves had been squeezed from the stone.
Try writing your words on pieces of stone or arranging them in stone patterns, spiralling on a pebble or in wavering strata-lines.

❖ Respond.  Now look at your stone words and write down how you react to those words.  What feelings or images do those words and the ideas behind them raise for you?  White chalk growing in a coral sea: undersea snow falls; frost shatters; stone heating, minerals migrating.

❖ Imaginative journeys.  Rocks are our main (our only?) source of information about the pre-human history of our planet.  It is rocks that invite us to picture the tropical seas that once laid down the chalk hills or the humid swamps that formed the coal measures.  The landscape holds the shapes scoured by glaciers.  Minerals and crystals are evidence of strange underground processes...

Use a rock to go on a trip to a place that no human has ever seen.  Immerse yourself in the place.  What can you see, feel, taste, smell?  Use these sensations to write a poem that holds the sensations of your visit.  You might shape it around those senses and then go further.

I see...

I feel...

I smell...

I hear...

I taste...

I remember...

I dream...

I am...

## Mighty mysterious microbes

Bacteria have been on this planet longer than any other living thing.  They are quite possibly the most successful life forms around us: they have outlasted everything else, they exist everywhere, and they are the beginning and the end of just about everything else.  They inhabit environments where other forms of life could not even begin to exist.  Mighty Mysterious Microbes sets out to explore our relationships with these wondrous creatures.

Working in a non-prescriptive way, this workshop on Mighty Mysterious Microbes tries to step away from moral environmental attitudes of 'good' and 'bad' and encourages a celebration of diversity, appreciating the inventiveness of nature and the connectedness of life. Designed as participatory theatre, this workshop is open-ended, encouraging a group to find its own information, understanding and final performance.

### Background

With your group, explore the roles of bacteria in our everyday lives. We are very used to having bacteria advertised as *'poisonous germs'* to be avoided and destroyed, so see how many other roles we can find for them from the flora of our digestive systems to the yeasts that ferment bread and rot fruit. Try looking at the world from a bacterial point of view.

### Conversations

Develop an exchange between bacteria and other life forms: you could even stage a debate about evolution and perhaps contributions to life on Earth. Bacteria might discuss their role in the development of the Earth, in the formation of soil, the ozone layer, and the atmosphere. Recycling, exchanging information, forming colonies, stromatolite cities... argue for a microbial civilization and see what happens.

### Research further

Look at bacteria population dynamics and think about how you might represent this dramatically, musically, verbally. Or look at images, use electron micrographs and photographs to explore the shapes of individuals and the patterns of colonies of microbes.

### How many forms of life?

Read a recent work on the diversity of life, discussing findings that throw our earlier assumptions about classifying the natural world into complete upheaval. The 3 kingdoms classically recognized are the plants, animals and fungi. Modern viewpoints, based on molecular evidence suggest that there may be as many as 30 bacteria kingdoms alone, each kingdom composed of organisms whose lives are as different from other bacterial kingdoms as plants are from animals.

As you start to accumulate information on your Mighty Microbes, your group could start thinking about ways of presenting this information in an exciting and accessible form for other people.

### Stories

Now move a little sideways and perhaps look at traditional stories. Exploring bacteria as Earth-builders you might find story ideas in tales of dragons and giants as Earth-shapers. Listen to the dramatic creation myths that revolve around the decay of a giant's body to build the ground beneath us. Listen to stories of fluids, as changing chimeras. Or even just look through the microbial kingdoms and find in miniature the monsters of older stories: hydras, harpies, Scylla and Charybdis may all be lurking at the bottom of a microscope.

Creativity

Rather than running through another list of activities here, you might turn to experiments with some of the activities outlined elsewhere in this work:

Shadow puppets;

Physical theatre and dance;

Story and voice;

Printed forms on cloth or paper.

## A blizzard of ideas

The outlines above show workshop patterns, building experiences through a range of activities.  These are just the beginning.  Deep Time/Deep Life ideas might prompt all sorts of imaginative ways of exploring complex issues.  Here follow a whirlwind of ideas.  They are simple sentences that might set you off.  Scribble in the margin.  Add your own.

Banners: fossils and the animals and plants they came from: *'life in ancient seas'*.

Make your own fossil: plaster casting with clay and shells and plastic animals' moulds.

Geological processes expressed through dance, drama and poetry.

Voices and/or music: look at the pace and rhythm of different processes: deep movement and sliding of one piece of Earth's crust over another in plate tectonics; fossilization through gradual decay; sedimentation, the slow building of layers and pressure; time, rocks folding and eroding, revelation; crystallization with flowing liquid magma, slow cooling at depth, the different crystallizing temperatures, shapes and colours of different minerals.

Use puppets to capture the characteristics of different rocks, minerals and crystals.

Tell stories inspired by the adventures of pebbles.  Write these on pebble outlines drawn on paper, reduce and reduce them again until you can fit a whole class worth onto a stone.  Or simply wrap your own stone story around the stone it came from.  (Thanks to Wesley Methodist Junior School).

Use tissue paper and PVA collage or painted glass to show crystal shapes and colours.

Solar systems and galaxies as painted glass or perspex mobiles, or even painted on clear glass baubles.

And so to begin.

Take a deep breath and plunge in with a smile and a light heart.

## Other contributors

The Mighty Mysterious Microbes section is based on the work of Ruth Brocklehurst.  She is an environmental artist *'fascinated by the processes of evolution, both physical and spiritual'* she is currently developing new ways of exploring life through performance.  Ruth can be contacted through the website of the arts and community group *'Elemental Earth'* at http://www.elementalearth.fslife.co.uk.

Susan Cross is a performance poet and environmental interpreter. She can be contacted at susan@telltale.co.uk.

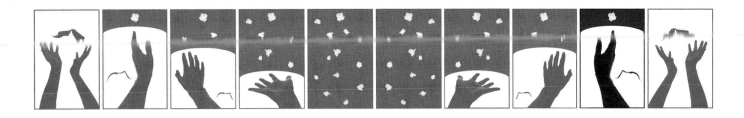

## Appendix 1:

# Tips for engaging on projects

Gordon MacLellan and Tom Mason

Here we offer guidelines to artists, teachers, parents and scientists who would like to embark on a project that explores the ideas and areas proposed in StarMatter. In setting up and letting loose your own art and science project; there are no definite answers here, only ideas. Advice relevant to one town may have no relevance in another country, or even in another region of the same country.

Rather than give a set of hard and fast answers to some of the questions you might ask yourself when planning a project, we have tried to distil some core qualities and principles that might help you in your planning.

Most of these responses are given as if you were planning for work in school but we hope there will be enough overlap with work based in museums and other education centres, or with holiday play schemes or weekly nature clubs – or wherever and whatever your situation – to be still useful.

### Why do this?

At the heart of StarMatter is the belief that only by developing and enriching our relationship with the natural world can we learn to live in a more positive way on this planet. To enable this development and enrichment through the understanding of scientific concepts and processes, we need to use creativity as much as formal teaching and traditional *'science'* lessons.

If you need to come up with reasons to justify your planned project, you might think about:

❖ Looking beyond the familiar: taking science teaching into new areas with new approaches.

❖ Embracing the dynamic nature of science: cosmology changes rapidly and ideas are evolving all the time. This makes the subjects of cosmology, astronomy, geology, palaeobiology very exciting to study. With that fluidity, why not explore it as much through art as through formal disciplines?

❖ Make science exciting!  Reminding people that science is about inspiration and imagination – combine learning and understanding with freedom of expression and we might produce a new wave of creative, thinking, dynamic students.

❖ A holistic approach encourages people to think creatively whatever the subject: help break the boxes that restrict our thinking, where we put art in one box, language in another, ecology in another and science some where else.

❖ Anchor our creativity in experience: working with Earth sciences in particular opens people up to whole realms of inspiration that is so unexpected.  The excitement of the stories that lie underneath our feet should not be overlooked.

❖ Widen our understanding of people: work with scientists and artists and see how these people work, think and are inspired.

❖ Creatively tackle our relationship with the planet we live on and the way in which we have affected it to date: rather than *'doom and gloom'*, attempting to celebrate and pro-actively address some of the issues raised by our sojourn on Earth.

## How do I start?

Ideally, we start with imagination, inspiration, the excitement to want to rush off and find things out, perhaps with a view to change; also the desire to look at stones and other elements of the planet we live on; the need to make things and tell people about them.

Assuming that that is there, maybe at the moment only in yourself, you may also need to think about practical things: how much time, money, materials and people have you got to work with?  Most of these areas will be returned to later.

Also, look at established parameters:

❖ Does this project need to fit into curriculum guidelines? If so, which ones?

❖ Do you have previous experience to draw upon?  Be aware however of not getting trapped into doing just what you have done before - take risks!

❖ Team work: what skills do you bring?  What sorts of outside people would it be good to work with?

Set some targets.

## Aims

Give yourself a clear aim and some objectives.  Clarity and simplicity are important.  Express objectives in terms of understanding, skills, awareness and confidence.  Distil each one to a single sentence.  Make sure it makes sense.  Ask if it is something you could in some way measure in its results.  Think about what you hope to achieve and the priorities within that.

## Participants

Who will participate in your project?  How many people, how old are they, where do they come from?  Can you find ways to widen participation in your project?  From a school, children might work with younger groups from a nursery and take them through some of the activities, or you might go to day-care centres and share experiences and activities, or listen to a local history group telling old stories from when, for example, quarries or mines were active in your neighbourhood.

## Evaluation

Not all objectives will give you measurable results.  Some will.  Some may match definite curriculum targets and can be measured in that way.  Others won't: don't expect all objectives to be strictly measurable.  If we are looking at opportunities for personal growth, change and inspiration, a lot of those things unfold slowly over time and cannot be pinned down to a box to be ticked.

However, we can ask each other as leaders how a project is progressing.  We can set up systems for our children to record their own feelings - for example, individual project journals with titles like *'My Journey to the Centre of the Earth'* and collective Scribble Sheets (ask a question and give groups seconds to scribble immediate responses) can help.  A slightly sideways evaluation comes with the numbers of parents who turn up for any finale: this is often a direct measure of the amount of talking about the work children have done when they got home.

## How much time will it take?

Oh dear.  How long is that piece of string?  How much time can you give?  For a minimal set of workshops you might allow a half-day – although a whole day is better – on a field trip or museum.  If working on a specific environmental project you may need more time to source research material and meet people with the right sort of experience.

Follow this up with some art workshops: perhaps three half days would give time for ideas to develop, some more research to be done and art work completed.

If several groups are working towards a finale, add a day for rehearsals and a final day for setting up and staging the finale.  Performance work takes longer.

Read through the Creeping Toad case study in an earlier section and see our thoughts there on the timing of that project.

## When to do this?

If you plan to work on geological field trips, plan for spring and summer. Autumn and winter in museums might be quieter than in the summer trip season and the staff may also have more spare time to help with the unusual workshops you need.

Don't forget that in some parts of the country people are very sensitive about apparent trespassing. Always seek permission, and follow the normal code of good country behaviour by walking round the edges of fields, and closing gates and leaving the animals in peace. Whether the animals will ignore you or not is another matter, as it is not unusual to be devotedly followed by curious heifers, or repeatedly butted by small stags. The only cure for the latter was a long wade through a swift stream, as he did not appear to like water!

It is also very important if you are planning to check a site out or visiting a quarry to make sure that someone knows where you are going, as even in big groups accidents can happen. In the UK, hard hats are compulsory headwear. Be especially careful on the coast as big waves can sneak up and soak you (or worse) while you are engrossed in what you are doing. It also does not do expensive cameras any good to be dunked in corrosive seawater.

It is essential that you know where you are, and if your climate is likely to be unpredictable, carry all of the gear that you may need in case of a sudden change. It is not funny or clever to be caught out without warm clothes, emergency food, and a means of making a fire. Learn to use a compass, map and Global Positioning System. Part of the attraction of outreach field trips is getting back to nature, but don't be foolish. Learn basic survival skills and be aware. You may think that you'll never need these skills, but an emergency in a wood in rural Ireland can be scary: in the great coniferous forests of Canada it can be life threatening.

## Finding things out

- ❖ Reference sources: we give some suggestions of books, websites, film and TV material in the Bibliography, Appendix II. We have given some ideas for areas of study/research in this document.

- ❖ Other people: look out local and national museums. A trip to your library could turn up geology, astronomy and natural history societies and associations. Check out local countryside or National Park ranger services and environmental education centres. You are looking for people who could provide information for you to work with and perhaps experts who could visit you or who could host a field visit by your group. Often local organizations can be more rewarding here than national ones: bigger groups often do not seem to have the time to spare while a local museum or park might be only too pleased to find someone interested in a slightly more unusual aspect of their work.

### People and more people – who can help?

Think about who you need to help you. Find out how much money they will cost! Overall, remember that you want people who can communicate effectively, as much as experts in their field. Amateurs can often be excellent sources of advice and help, and are often as knowledgeable as the experts. They may be even better at explaining their local knowledge, as they have learned it by hands-on experience.

Depending upon how you are structuring your project, this research might need to be done in advance or you might like to work with your group to decide what sort of people they feel they need to meet. They could then track down and contact these various experts themselves.

Just like medical advice, always try to seek a second opinion. Artists, naturalists and scientists are often opinionated and argumentative, but they are not always right. Make sure to think critically about what you are being told, and keep your sceptical filters well cleaned and ready for action. It is often very instructive to have the learning benefit of listening to two experts arguing at the scene, but make sure that you ask them to explain themselves if they lapse into jargon and acronyms.

Some scientists are quite comfortable to drift into the arts as they may well have been using visualization methods for years. Their notebooks are sometimes well illustrated with small works of art. Note the success of amateur naturalists' notebooks, published as small snapshots of Edwardian or Victorian leisurely lifestyles.

### Finding artists

Approach your local authority Arts Officer for suggestions or talk to other schools and play schemes about people they have worked with in the past.

In Britain, the Ashden Trust runs a Directory of Environmental Theatre Groups to be found at *http://www.ashdendirectory.org.uk/editor/thetrust.html* but in Ireland, Regional Arts Boards are probably the best starting point for lists of artists working with different media.

Then there are arts centres, writing and poetry groups, art galleries, museums, parks and anywhere that might bring people in to lead workshops.

### Finding scientists and other experts

Museums and local natural history or conservation organizations are good starting points. Your nearest university would be worth talking to and perhaps a national geological or astronomical association. A library might introduce you to local astronomers or geologists and others. For experts working on environmental strategies and practices, contact your local environmental education centre.

## Places to go

As with people: explore and experiment. The same venues that yielded
scientists might offer exciting places to visit. Be open to unexpected
possibilities. In UK there are *'sites of special scientific interest'* and even at
least one World Heritage Site identified because of their geological value.
The more important a site, the more you will have to share it with others.
It is absolutely forbidden to sample at many of these sites, so you will need
to develop your sketching and note taking skills or to be able to take a good
photograph that will capture the essence of the place.

Get into the aesthetics of composition of a good photograph: it is easy to
take a hurried snap, but actually making the image a picture that is worth
a thousand words is a hard learned skill. The advent of high resolution,
relatively cheap digital cameras means that it is easier now to check the
image before you move on, so the *'perfect'* image is theoretically available
to all. In practice, it means that we are even more profligate with the
numbers of images taken. But do a ruthless edit before you clog up your
computer's hard drive with electronic image garbage.

This is another way of looking at the art science interface, and many find
that the use of digital cameras is a liberating experience in its own right.
With some good software, images can be burnished to perfection, but
beware of overkill. Keep it simple.

Outdoor visits might not offer the breadth of resources that a museum or
planetarium could offer, but they would take your group to *'wild'* rocks, to
places where they could see and feel and get a taste of the processes that
shape the stone around us. These places let us meet rocks under the open
sky or under ground in caves – and that contact with living rock can lend a
whole new set of inspirations to our work. This is enormously important:
we are part of the wild planet; our civilization is a paper-thin veneer: so
satisfy that deeply rooted urge to get out and feel the wind and smell the
snow.

There are organizations that have developed sustainable strategies in the
USA. While these may be too far away to visit from Ireland, they have
good websites and may be open to queries from interested groups, especially
those working on projects linked with the arts. You can often find
inspirational material at these sites, but beware of sites that are
pseudoscience, they are very common, and often cloaked in respectability.
Keep to the well-known university and museum sites, and it is likely that
their links will be to reputable sites with a credible record, and staff who
have written the material.

## Newspapers

Talk to your local media. We are playing with interesting ideas here, *'the history of the world from the Big Bang to the Millennium Dome'*, *'stones have adventures too'* and *'the story of life and its relationship with the planet'* sort of stuff. Try to have a small article or short interview published early on in the project and see if this prompts your neighbourhood recluse to step forward and reveal a wondrous geology collection for your use: or a telescope tuned in and pointing and open for an evening of stargazing.

Good starting points are to use the journalistic method to tell your story, and/or to plan its development. What happened? When? Where? Why would anyone else be interested? Selling concepts in words, spoken or written, is a bit like selling a house; you have a very small time in which to make your first impression. You must get it right then, or the cause is lost and you will have lost your reader or your audience's interest. If you start by thinking that something is very interesting, be sure to conduct a reality check that it is truly going to be of interest to others. It is then up to you to transform the idea into reality.

## But what should we do?   Subjects and artforms

The range of ideas involved in understanding our relationship with our planet is bewilderingly diverse. A single project could easily lose itself in being spread too thin and trying to catch a bit of everything. It is therefore worth picking up a single thread and working with that: the Solar System, perhaps, or ancient life and the messages it holds, or geological history and processes.

A decision here might be informed by:

* ❖ Resources available in your school and local area: people to work with, places to visit.

* ❖ Previous work: do not just repeat work done before, but build upon it so that your group members bring some knowledge with them, rather than being thrown completely into unknown territory. The artforms that you could use to explore this topic often suggest themselves as you start to pin subject areas down. Think about the nature of the topic you hope to explore.

* ❖ Processes and timescales might lend themselves to movement, music and song.

* ❖ Things with specific characteristics might suggest puppet, mask or story characters.

* ❖ The colours of planets, space (those Hubble Telescope pictures!), crystals and the shapes of fossils, might lend themselves to printing.

But perhaps go with what inspires you, even if it seems unlikely. Or talk to artists you feel comfortable with and see what starting points they bring. Remember that apparently separate will work together (printed star cloths could become dance performances for example). When your project is up and running your group might well have their own ideas about how they would like to express their discoveries and your careful plans about what would be produced might need to be changed. Try to respect the group's creativity and find ways of integrating different ideas into a final performance, exhibition or whatever.

Remember your audience. If your listeners or observers don't know a bedpost from a brachiopod, it is part of your mission to have them sitting on the edge of their seats while you carry them into their own understanding of the marvels of the brachiopod world.

## Who will give us some money?

The criteria organizations use in funding projects change regularly and what we might suggest one year might be out of date by the next or inapplicable elsewhere. So rather than giving a list of people to approach, here we would suggest some of the criteria you might apply to a StarMatter project.

Think of a StarMatter project as offering some of the following:

❖ Sustainability-centred work that also draws in ideas about culture and the relationship between people and places and how people use their environment.

❖ Inspiring science: there are often funds available for promoting innovative ways of making science accessible.

❖ Personal, school and community development, through new skills and new understandings and the value of personal interpretations of the world we live in. A project might also work across community groups, working in and out of school, bringing other residents into school to share knowledge and experience.

❖ Combining science with specific artforms: words, dance, drama.

❖ Exploring the local area/heritage: an understanding of local landscape and geology; how it has been, is being and could be used by people.

❖ What area do we cover? Consider whether you are approaching this as predominantly.

❖ An arts project (and if so is it visual or audio performance, literary or mixed media?), a science project or a mixed science/arts project?

❖ An environmental initiative, looking at the processes that give us the landscapes we live in, and the environmental consequences of those?

❖ A sustainability project?

Each of these areas might open up different sources of funding.

## Clarity

Do think carefully about your project; do not try to call it too many different things to too many different funding sources/people. Clarity and simplicity are still important. Go back to those earlier notes about aims, objectives and participants. Think about what you hope to achieve and the priorities within that and this should help you set off down a relevant funding avenue. Recognize that your ideas might need to be refined to fit funding criteria.

## Looking for funding

Start by talking to people. There should be people in your local authority who could suggest sources of money to you. In the UK, Regional Arts Boards and other venues usually hold copies of '*Funder Finder*', an interactive database where you enter the parameters of your project and the database feeds back suggestions of organizations to approach. Most importantly, give yourself lots of time if you are going to be chasing funding.

## Finding resources: geological and other supplies

Try your local school suppliers for sets of rocks, information on planets, etc. Also, search the Internet.

Useful UK sources include:

❖ Northern Geological Supplies: *www.norgeo.co.uk/inside/catalogue.htm*.

❖ Phillip Harris: *www.phscientific.co.uk*.

❖ Geo Supplies Ltd: www.geosupplies.co.uk. Geo Supplies also publish the useful geology newspaper '*Down to Earth*'.

❖ NES Arnold (for art and science supplies): *www.nesarnold.co.uk*.

## Art materials

Your regular school supplier should give you most of what you need. If you are not a school, explore that system and buy larger quantities of paint, glue etc. It is usually much more cost effective than buying lots of small quantities from art supply shops.

## Scrap stores

Find out where, if anywhere, your nearest Play Resources Warehouse or '*Scrap Store*' is. These wonderful establishments usually provide basic materials at competitive rates. But the real richness of their resource comes with the safe industrial waste they source and redistribute: foam rubber, plastic bottles, strange lumpy bits of stuff, chunks of wax, rolls of cloth, tubs of glittery baubles.

Scrap Stores can look like a post-apocalyptic Aladdin's Cave: go with a reliable friend who will drag you out if you get too excited!  Track them down through a library, play scheme or youth group, or through whichever branch of your local authority deals with children and play schemes.

It is also worth finding out who else is visiting, if you find your treasure there, like-minded scavengers will be hunting through the discarded gems too.  During the summer, the staff of the Armagh Planetarium collect Play Resources warehouse stuff to make rockets and aliens, and draw the moon and the sun and the stars.  In the case of the planetarium, the sky is no limit.

## Making it happen

Here are a few suggestions for starting to look at some of the subjects we have explored in this project through art and drama work.

❖ Start with the personal: carefully examine the rock and mineral specimens, shells, fossils, fungi people have collected and places that they have visited.  Remember to check water resources and larger geological features that they remember or have visited; even *'bugs'* they may have had on holiday: why, what is special?

❖ Be active: make your special stones, planets and other geological features out of people; roll around the floor: perform your geology as soon as possible.

❖ Think of geological processes as lifecycles: the pulse of the planet beats so slowly that we may appear to be hyperactive fleas on a Lovelock-described Gaian timescale.  Earth abides, despite us.

❖ Tell lifecycles as stories: they have action, stillness, passion and tension... use the timescales of stones for extra effect.

❖ Remember cosmological and geological life cycles are ever so much slower than our own: *"The pebble I hold in my hand is older than the mountain behind me"*.  In many places pebbles may be extremely old, in parts of Africa, rocks over 3 billion years old are commonplace, but when deciphered they reveal a world as alien as Mars will appear to the first explorers.

❖ As your group does more research have information available for individuals or pairs of students: better lots of cheap postcards than one big book per class.

❖ Keep terminology familiar: use words like *'appearance'*, *'behaviour'*. Use this information to build character profiles and even puppets of different stones, minerals, rocks, planets and life-forms: add in history, relationships, aims, write the story of what might happen next to that mineral, planet or life-form on a human timescale and on a geological timescale.

❖ Recognize the risk of anthropomorphism (making it all too *'human'*) but those familiar terms can bring geology to life for your group.

❖ Come back to stones, life and people: where might we meet this rock or that stone; this crystal or that fungus; this rock formation or that meteorite.

❖ Don't get trapped by dinosaurs. If looking at prehistoric life, try plunging into the amazing Precambrian and Palaeozoic seas! Look back for the Origin of Life.

❖ Aim as much for excitement and enthusiasm as precise factual accuracy: understanding can grow and change, but enthusiasm is needed first!

## Managing the company

The ideas in *'Making it happen'* include elements of how you work with and respond to your company. Other things to consider might include:

❖ Talk as a company: stop and review together. Get people to talk to each other about what they have done and where things should or could go next. Listen to these ideas and use them. Make the project collective rather than prescriptive.

❖ Talk as workshop leaders: a wind-down at the end of new activity work shops is always helpful. Try to do this without pointing fingers or taking comments personally, but listen to what worked, what didn't work. When did we all miss the point completely?

❖ Don't be afraid of repeating discussions with the whole company on another day. Take time to reinforce ideas and renew inspiration, even if you have to let go of some of the new things you hoped to do. It will be better for your company to be rooted and confident in their own interpretative ability than advancing too fast and stumbling over things that they do not understand.

❖ Listen to everyone: are we on the same wavelength... or at least on the same planet or in the same time period?

## Other ideas

This is an assortment of brainstorm ideas from the StarMatter team. However, if you have time, why not do an inspirations brainstorm with your group to see how many ideas you can come up with. It is easy to get very carried away...

❖ Evolution of life: with shadow puppets.

❖ Banners: fossils and the animals and plants they came from.

❖ Make your own fossil: plaster casting with clay and shells and plastic animal moulds.

❖ Geological processes expressed through dance, drama and poetry.

❖ Characterization to represent elements of our life-support system and the effects we as humans have on them.

❖ Voices and/or music: look at the pace and rhythm of different processes: deep movement and sliding of one piece of Earth's crust over another in plate tectonic processes; fossilization through gradual decay and chemical change; sedimentation, the slow building of layers and increasing pressure; time; rocks folding; metamorphic recrystallization; slow cooling at depth and crystallization from liquid magma; the different crystallizing temperatures; shapes and colours of different minerals.

## What next?

Plan as far as you can.  Recruit people and track down resources.  Your planning will never be perfect.  You will probably never find all that you might need, or source all that you want.  It is more important to act. Embark on the adventure with your group and know that there will be new experiences for all of you.

Take a deep breath and plunge in with a smile and a light heart.

Breath from the Voice touches dust

And life rises slowly out from the sea

Great monsters and creatures

Crawl out on dry land,

Some take to the air with their wings.

*Extract from class poem by pupils*
*of the Wesley Methodist Primary School,*
*Buxton, Derbyshire, UK.*

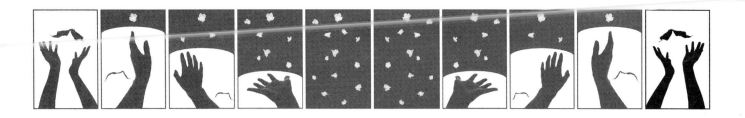

## Appendix 2:

# Biographies and Bibliography

## Biographies

### LESLIE BROWN

Leslie Brown is an artist with a background in social science and an interest in bridge-building between Arts and Sciences - facilitating children within the workshop module in particular.

### GAVIN FRANKEL

Gavin Frankel grew up in rural Ireland, a time and place that has ever since been a source of inspiration to him. He studied law at university, followed by a photography course in Paris. He was taught by the master printer George Fevre. When he returned to Ireland he held a successful exhibition of his street photography, images of everyday life in Paris. Frankel's first professional commission was to photograph 800 old houses for the National Architectural Archives. He then went to Dublin and began to photograph fashion and portraits. His second exhibition featured aspects of Irish country life: portraits and landscapes. Frankel then married and went to live in Seoul, South Korea for two years. He started to work for magazines, photographing architecture, fashion and travel stories. He has recently returned to Europe and has settled in Paris with his wife and daughter.

Exhibitions of his personal work include:
Paris Street Scenes (Cork 2000);
Faces (Dublin 2001);
Bamboo Forest By Night (London 2003).

## GORDON MACLELLAN

Gordon MacLellan has been described as one of Britain's leading environmental educators. As *'Creeping Toad'*, Gordon works with groups to find ways of celebrating the relationships between people and the places where they live and work and play.  He has a reputation for creating settings where people can challenge themselves, learning new skills, renewing their connection with the world and stepping beyond perceived limitations to dance, tell stories, lead processions, perform with puppets... Gordon's work is increasingly international with work in Slovakia, South Africa and the USA in recent years.

He is well-known as a trainer and writer, with three books in print; *Talking to the Earth* and *Sacred Animals* (both published by Capall Bann) and *The Piatkus Guide to Shamanism*, (Piatkus). He is currently working on Celebrating Nature, a manual for creating community celebrations

Gordon is a trained ecologist and experienced teacher.

With an additional background as an artist, storyteller, puppeteer and dancer, his work in celebrations allows him to combine both scientific and expressive fields to create exceptional situations for the groups he works with.

## TOM MASON

Dr. Tom Mason is a geologist. He trained at the Queen's University of Belfast, and spent 22 years in South Africa teaching at the University of KwaZulu Natal in Durban. He has extensive experience as a geological research professor, working on palaeontological topics ranging from the description of the earliest fossils on Earth to mammal-like reptiles of the Karoo and using their trace fossils to describe ancient environments.

Having returned to Ireland in 1996 to take up his present post as Director of the Armagh Planetarium. He set up and trained the Planetarium's team of Educational Outreach staff who now provide a curriculum-broadening programme that is available to all schools and community groups throughout Ireland. He has worked with all age groups, has run science training workshops for Primary and Special Needs teachers and regularly presents interactive science workshops at special needs schools.

Tom Mason sees his prime function as spreading the knowledge that science is in a constant state of flux which makes it a fun topic to study and enjoy.

## CHRIS VIS

Chris Vis studied at the Royal College of Art, the Hague, Holland. After a career in advertising in Dublin he became Head of Art at St. Columba's College, Co. Dublin, till his retirement in 2001. For the last 12 years he has been the Visiting Examiner for Art in Ireland for the International Baccalaureate Organisation.

He has a special interest in the value of Art within the larger educational framework.

# Bibliography

## Books

Alexandersson, Olof. 1990. *Living Water: Viktor Schauberger and the secrets of natural energy.* Revised edition. (Gateway Books, Bath).

Allègre, Claude. 1992. *From Stone to Star: A View of Modern Geology.* (Harvard University Press, Cambridge, Massachusetts).

Anderson, L. 1999. *Genetic Engineering, Food, and our Environment: a Brief Guide.* (Green Books, Dartington, Devon).

Baillie, Mike. 1999. *Exodus to Arthur: Catastrophic Encounters with Comets.* (B. T. Batsford Ltd., London).

Berry, T. 1999. *The Great Work.* (Bell Tower, New York).

Berry, Thomas. 1988. *The Dream of the Earth.* (Sierra Club Books, San Francisco).

Boal, A. 1982. *The Theatre of the Oppressed. Second edition.* (Routledge Press, London).

Boal, A. 1992. *Games for Actors and Non-Actors.* (Routledge Press, New York).

Bochenek, V. 1996. *Le Mime Marcel Marceau – Entretiens et regards avec Valerie Bochenek.* (Somogy Editions d'Art, Paris).

Booth, Basil. 1997. *Identifying Rocks and Minerals.* (Apple, London).

Boyle, Godfrey (ed.). 1998. *Renewable Energy – Power for a Sustainable Future.* (Oxford University Press, Oxford).

Button, J. (ed.). 1991. *The Best of Resurgence.* (Lilliput, Dublin).

Bynum, W. F., Browne, E. J. & Porter, R. (eds). 1981. *The Macmillan Dictionary of the History of Science.* (Macmilllan, London).

Campbell, J. 1988. *The Power of Myth.* (Doubleday, New York).

Capra, Fritjof. 1983. *The Tao of Physics. Revised edition.* (Flamingo Books, London).

Carson, Rachel. 2000. *Silent Spring.* (Penguin Classics, London).

Cassidy J. 1994. *Earthsearch – A Kids' Geography Museum in a Book.* (Palo Alto, Klutz).

Cornell, J. 1989. *Sharing the Joy of Nature.* (Dawn Publications, Nevada City).

Cornell, Joseph. 1998. *Sharing Nature with Children. 2nd edition* (Dawn Publications, Nevada City).

Couper, Heather & Henbest, Nigel. 1991. *Big Bang.* (DK Publishing, New York).

Davies, Paul. 1990. *God and the New Physics.* (Penguin Books, London).

Davies, Paul. 1994. *The Edge of Infinity.* (Penguin Books, London).

Davies, Paul. 1995. *Superforce. Revised edition.* (Penguin Books, London) revised edition.

Davies, Paul. 1999. *The Fifth Miracle: The Search for the Origin of Life.* (Penguin Books, London). Reprinted 2003 with updates and revised title, *The Origin of Life.*

Davies, Paul & Gribbin, John. 1992. *The Matter Myth: Beyond Chaos and Complexity.* (Penguin Books, London).

De Lage, C. R. 2000. *Intérieur Rue Christophe Raynaud de Lage – 10 ans de théâtre de rue (1989-1999).* (Editions théâtrales, Paris).

Dixon, Dougal. 2000. *Beginner's Guide to Geology.* (Chancellor Press, London).

Douthwaite, Richard. 1999. *The Ecology of Money.* (Green Books, Dartington, Devon).

Dunning, F. W., Mercer, I. F., Owen, M. P., Roberts, R. H. & Lambert, J. L. M. 1978. *Britain before Man.* (Institute of Geological Sciences, London).

Elkington, John. 1999. *Cannibals with Forks.* (Capstone, Oxford).

Elkington, John & Hailes, Julia. 1991. *The Green Business Guide.* (Victor Gollancz, London).

Fejer, Frampton & Fitzsimons. 1997. *Rocks and Minerals.* (Brockhampton Press, London).

Feynman, Richard. 1998. *The Meaning of it all.* (Penguin Books, London).

Feynman, Richard. 1992. *"Surely you are joking Mr Feynman."* (Vintage, London).

Feynman, Richard. 1990. *QED: The Strange Theory of Light and Matter.* (Penguin Books, London).

Fortey, Richard.  1998.  *Life: The Unauthorised Biography.*  (Flamingo, London).

Fortey, Richard.  2000.  *Trilobite: Eyewitness to Evolution.*  (Harper Collins, London).

Fortey, Richard.  2004.  *The Earth an intimate history.*  (Harper Collins, Publishers).

Fry, Norman.  1992.  *The Field Description of Metamorphic Rocks.*  (John Wiley, Chichester).

Gamow, George.  1993.  *Mr Tompkins* (Paperback).  (Cambridge University Press, Cambridge).

Garlick, Judy (ed.).  1996.  *Atlas of Earthcare.*  (Gaia Books, London).

Gee, Henry.  2000.  *Deep Time: Cladistics: the revolution in Evolution.* (Fourth Estate, London).

Gee, Henry.  2001.  *Deep Time.*  (Fourth Estate, London).

Gilpin, Alan.  1996.  *A Dictionary of the Environment and Sustainable Development.*  (John Wiley & Sons, Chichester).

Giradet, Herbert.  1999.  *Creating Sustainable Cities.*  (Green Books, Dartington, Devon).

Gleick, James.  1994.  *Genius: Richard Feynman and Modern Physics.* (Abacus, London).

Hawken, Paul, Lovins, A. B. &  Lovins, L. H.  1999.  *Natural Capitalism.* (Little Brown & Co., Santa Fe).

Hawking, Stephen.  2001.  *The Universe in a Nutshell.*  (Bantam Press, London).

Hunken, Jorie & The New England Wild Flower Society.  1989.  *Botany for all Ages.*  (The Globe Pequot Press, Connecticut).

Kains, M. G.  1973.  *Five Acres and Independence.*  (Dover Publications, New York).

Kumar, Satish.  1992.  *No Destination. 2nd Edition.*  (Resurgence Books, Dartington, Devon).

Kunzig, Robert.  2000.  *Mapping the Deep: The Extraordinary Story of Ocean Science.*  (Sort of Books, London).

Lalli, Carol M. & Parsons, Timothy R.  1993.  *Biological Oceanography: An Introduction. 2nd Edition.*  (Butterworth-Heinemann, Oxford).

Lamb, Simon & Sington, David.  1998. *The Earth story: The shaping of our world.*  (BBCE Books, London).

Lang, Peter.  1996.  *Ethical Investment: A Saver's guide.*  (Jon Carpenter, Kent).

Legaut, Charlotte. 2000. *Recreation.* (Editions du rouer gue, Rodez).

Liebes, Sidney, Sahtouris, Elisabet, & Swimme, Brian. 1998. *A walk through time.* (John Wiley & Sons, New York).

Lonergan, Anne & Richards, Caroline (eds). 1987. *Thomas Berry and the New Cosmology.* (Twenty Third Publications, Mystic, Connecticut).

Lovelock, James. 1995. *Gaia: a practical science of planetary Medicine.* (Oxford University Press, Oxford) revised.

Luoma, Jon R. 1999. *The Hidden Forest: The Biography of an Ecosystem.* (Henry Holt & Company, New York).

McDonagh, Sean. 1986. *To care for the Earth.* (Geoffrey Chapman, London).

McDonagh, Sean. 1994. *Passion for the Earth.* (Geoffrey Chapman, London).

MacLellan, Gordon. 1995. *Talking to the Earth.* (Capall Bann Publishing, Freshfields, Berks).

MacLellan, Gordon. 1997. *Sacred Animals.* (Capall Bann Publishing, Freshfields, Berks).

Macagno, Gilles. 1999. *Une Histoire de la Vie.* (Ellipses, Paris).

Meyer, Aubrey. 2000. *Contraction and Convergence.* (Green Books, Dartington, Devon).

Milbrath, Lester W. 1996. *Learning to think Environmentally.* (SUNY Press, Albany, New York).

Murphy, Brendan & Nance, Damian. 1999. *Earth Science Today.* (International Thomson Publishing, London).

Myers, Norman (ed.). 1993. *Gaia: An atlas of planet management.* (Anchor Books, London).

Natural History Museum, The. 1991. *The Story of the Earth.* (British Museum Publications, London).

Natrass, Brian & Altomare, Mary. 1999. *The Natural Step for Business.* (New Society Publishers, British Columbia).

Norman, David. 1994. *Prehistoric Life.* (Macmillan, New York).

Palmer, Douglas. 1999. *Encyclopaedia of Dinosaurs and Prehistoric Animals.* (Marshall Publishing, London).

Robertson, James. 1998. *Transforming Economic Life A Millennial Challenge.* (Green Books, Dartington, Devon).

Russell, Peter. 2000. *The Global Brain Awakens: Our Next Evolutionary Leap.* (Element Books, Shaftesbury, Dorset).

Ryan, William & Pitman, Walter. 1999. *Noah's Flood.* (Simon and Schuster, London).

Schumacher, E. F. 1993. *Small is Beautiful.* (Vintage, London).

Schumacher, E. F. 1996. *This I Believe.* (The Schumacher Society, Dartington).

Shepherd, Allan. 1996. *Careers and Courses in Sustainable Technologies.* (CAT books, Centre of Alternative Technology Powys).

Smillie, Joe & Gershuny, Grace. 1999. *The Soul of Soil. 4th Edition.* (Chelsea Green, Vermont).

Stannard, Russell. 1994. *Uncle Albert and the Quantum Quest.* (Faber and Faber, London).

Steingraber, Sandra. 1999. *Living Downstream.* (Virago Books, London).

Stott, Robert. 2000. *Schumacher Briefing – The Ecology of Health.* (Green Books, Dartington, Devon).

Sussman, Art. 2000. *Dr Art's Guide to Planet Earth.* (Chelsea Green, White River Junction Vermont).

Swimmc, Brian. 1984. *The Universe is a Green Dragon.* (Bear and Co., Santa Fe).

Swimme, Brian. 1996. *The Hidden Heart of the Cosmos.* (Orbis books, New York).

Swimme, Brian & Berry, Thomas. 1994. *The Universe Story.* (Harper Collins, New York).

Thomas, Lewis. 1978. *The Lives of the Cell.* (Penguin Books, London).

Thorpe, Richard & Brown, Geoff. 1993. *The Field Description of Igneous Rocks.* (John Wiley, Chichester).

Tudge, C. 2002. *The Variety of Life.* (Oxford University Press, Oxford).

Tudge, C. 2002. *Fragments of Life.* (BBC Wildlife Magazine, August 2002, London).

Wackernagel, Mathis & Rees, William. 1996. *Our Ecological Footprint.* (New Society, Gabriola Island, British Columbia).

Weisman, Alan. 1998. *Gaviotas.* (Chelsea Green Publishing, White River Junction, Vermont).

Von Weizacker, Ernst, Lovins, Amory B. & Lovins, L. Hunter. 1998. *Factor Four: Doubling Wealth, Halving Resource Use.* (Earthscan, London).

Whitefield, Patrick. 1993. *Permaculture in a Nutshell.* (Permanent Publications, East Meon).

Wilson, Edward O. 1998. *Consilience: The Unity of Knowledge.* (Abacus, London).

Woodcock, Nigel & Strachan, Rob (eds). 2000. *Geological History of Britain and Ireland.* (Blackwell Science, London).

Woods, Caoimhin & Philips, Davie. 2000. *Source Book 2000.* (United Spirit Books, Dublin).

Wooley, Tom (ed.). 1997. *Green Building Handbook.* (EF and Spoon, London).

Zukav, Gary. 1979. *The Dancing Wu Li Masters.* (William Morrow, New York).

## Audio resources

MacGillis, Miriam Therese. *To Know the Place for the First Time: Explorations in Thomas Berry's New Cosmology.*
(Sonoma: Global Perspectives).

MacGillis, Miriam Therese. *Earth Economy, Human Economy – closing the gap.*
(Sonoma: Global Perspectives).

MacGillis, Miriam Therese. *From Alienation to Unity.*
(Genesis Farm).

MacGillis, Miriam Therese. *Global Education.*
(Genesis Farm).

Swimme, Brian. *Canticle to the Cosmos.*
(Boulder: Sounds True Audio, 1995).

## Film and video resources

*Ancient Futures: Learning from Ladakh.* John Page
(International Society for Ecology and Culture).

*Answers about Gaia.* James Lovelock.
(Schumacher College).

*Blue Planet.* Alistair Fothergill (BBCE).

*Deep Answers.* Arne Naess.
(Schumacher College).

*Ecological Economics.* J. Robertson & R. Douthwaite.
(Schumacher College).

*Ecology, Theology and Soul.* T. Berry & T. Moore.
(Schumacher College).

*Economics and Globalisation.*  M. Khor & R. Sandbrook.
 (Schumacher College).

*Global Power, Local Promise.*  H. Nodge, W. Sachs & M. Wackernagel.
 (Schumacher College).

*Mind and Matter.*  S. Kumar, B. Goodwin & D. Peat.
 (Schumacher College).

*Natural Capitalism.*  A. Lovins & J. Elkington.
 (Schumacher College).

*Permaculture in Practice.*  Michael Baldwin.
 (Iota Pictures 1996).

*Questions about Gaia.*  James Lovelock.
 (Schumacher College).

*SolarMax.*  John Wiley.
 (Museum of Science and Industry).

*Women & Ecology.*  W. Laduke & W. Harcourt.
 (Schumacher College).

*Written in Stone.*  Gillian Marsh.
 (RTE and Videogram, 1996).


## Useful magazines and journals

*Earthlight.*

*Ecologist, The.*

*Gaia Circular.*

*Nature, London.*

*New Scientist.*

*Ocean Arks Annals of the Earth.*

*Permaculture Magazine.*

*Positive News.*

*Resurgence.*

*Watershed Sentinel, The.*

Time moves slowly.

The smallest survive and walk from their caves;

When the sun shows her face again.

With rocks in their hands;

With dreams in their minds;

They build a great city of stone.

Empires are built and battles are fought,

Each nation then has its own voice.

But the voice of the maker is written on stone,

And is smashed on a mountain by man.

*Extract from class poem by pupils*
*of the Wesley Methodist Primary School,*
*Buxton, Derbyshire, UK.*

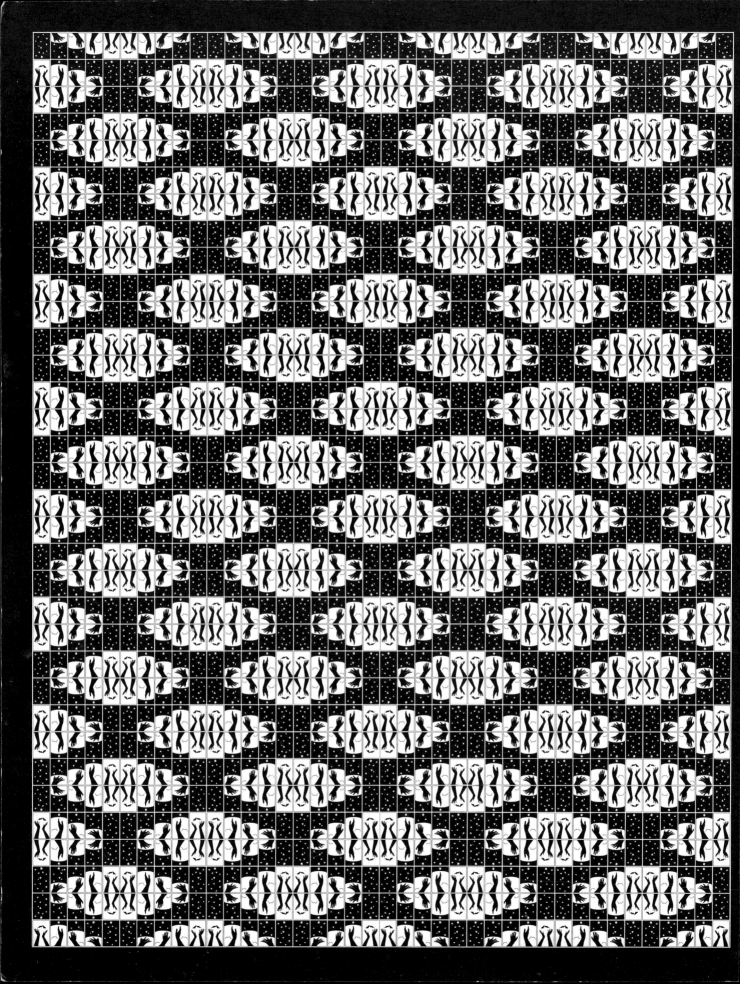